Prais

Be A High Achiever is a must read for every student. It indeed provides excellent principles and step-by-step tools in how students can be successful in their academic life and beyond.

~ Purita Bristow,
former Assistant Director of
Information Systems Services,
University of Windsor

This book is for any student who has ever wondered how to succeed at college or university. Written in a straightforward style, Franklin outlines everything you need to know and do – from setting goals and studying 'smart' to having fun in and out of school. This is a handy gift for all students.

~ Akin Taiwo,
Assistant Professor, Western
University

All readers, whatever your level of college and university education will find a lot of strategies and ideas to stimulate your goals achievement and help you effectively maximize your time at school. You owe it to yourself to read this outstanding book as its breath and scope, the variety of data explored, and the stark nature of the argument will provoke you to think very clearly in becoming the best you can ever dream to be.

~ Dr. Irene Popoola,
C.E.O Oasis Educational Resource
Ltd

I wish I had read this book years ago as a university student instead of having to read it to write an endorsement to it. When you do not know where you are going everywhere looks like it. Yet you cannot win the educational game (or that of life for that matter) without a game plan. Here is an academic game plan in a book form.

~ Albert Oduwole,
International Conference
Speaker and Author

BE A
HIGH
ACHIEVER

ACHIEVING ALL-ROUND SUCCESS
IN COLLEGE & UNIVERSITY

FRANKLIN H. EZENWA

I dedicate this book to my lovely parents, Edwin and Catherine Ezenwa, for their selfless love and sacrifice towards my siblings and me; I appreciate both of you. Also, to everyone who will benefit from this book;

I wish you the best. Finally, to my Creator and Source of inspiration; I appreciate You.

CONTENTS

Part 3: Approaching the finish line

Foreword

At every university open house, I still meet new applicants who are going to be the first in their family to enter post-secondary education. It equally surprises me when I encounter the other extreme where over achieving parents are dragging their "child" to start a career at the university, the one that they picked for him or her. Both cases have common attributes: there is no question that their freshmen year will be quite a challenge. They are at risk students from the onset where I see the need for academic counselling in their near future. It needs not to be this way.

The case of the motivated freshman who may have all the love and support of the parents, how well-prepared will they face the new-found freedom and independence of university life? How well will they recover from the shock of a failed midterm grade? I happen to fall into that category, and I attest that the first year was my most challenging year. Needless to say, with a lot of personal effort, sleepless nights and starvation, I managed to pass my courses. It was not until the third year that I started learning about strategically scheduling my time, effective strategies to approach studying for exams; and of course, prioritizing my finances now that my debt from student loans had exceeded my nurturing parents' savings. I often wished that someone would have told me about these things sooner; particularly how I could have avoided falling into these holes so I would not have to waste my better energy in digging myself out. The little tricks that make you go the distance I suppose, or this little catalyst that would have made my efforts more productive in attaining the grade I needed within acceptable mental and physical limits. This book is long overdue, but never too late to the new recruits. Here you will find the do's and don'ts of college & university life, a smarter way to set and see your goals through without draining your mental, physical, social and financial life.

Then there is the spoiled child scenario – at least in the eyes of the parents – who are used to taking care for their child's every need, having him or her take things for granted and never had to worry about the real world. There is no shortage of millennials falling into this category, and that real-world shock can be quite dreadful. Those are the ones with often educated parents who are used to providing everything for their offspring. At my last encounter with one of these students I uncovered a startling reality - inside this "careless person" there is a voice crying for help, a person in the background who is quite intelligent but often suppressed and lacked the opportunity to express. I quickly turn a brief encounter into an advising session, and in my mind, I am going through the "ABC's" of this book... the basics of handling independence, time organization, academic as well as non-academic life all around. For this person, this book is an investment not only to academic success but also to personal enrichment.

Franklin's style presents a warm personal hand to hold along the path of academic success. He is not afraid to warn of the many pitfalls that he encountered or the challenges that one would face. It is the voice of experience that shaped the wisdom of this book. As I read the book, I couldn't help but reflect back on my own experiences. To me, I may argue that "oh yes, of course, that's what I would do too," but with one heart-aching regret: "I wish I knew these sooner rather than later, instead of learning the hard way." It is very critical to learn the wisdom of others who took the path before us. While there are many books on self-help and success at the college & university, they often carry the voice of the parent's generation and their experiences, something a millennial would have a hard time relating to. There is a fresh approach in Franklin's voice – it carries the feel of a trusted roommate having a frank discussion, or a friend reflecting on his own experience, either way, it is an honest, first-person, tested and validated anecdote.

Finally, success is not guaranteed, nor is failure an option when one builds on a solid path. Personal confidence, maturity and paying attention to the goals that matter the most all contribute their adopters to leap into the path of success. It is necessary to fail, however, to learn not to repeat a mistake, but at the same time, a piece of advice can go a long way in helping the fallen to get back up quickly. Franklin's academic and career success is a repeated story that I have witnessed over the years by many computer science graduates. It is the typical story that needs to be told - the smart, strategic student who lands a dream job before graduation. Many are busy enjoying their success afterwards, while Franklin took the time to tell his account for the multitude to follow this path. To every student from every walk of life, if you are thinking about studying computer science in particular or just exploring the strategies to succeed in your post-secondary adventure, this book is for you.

> Dr. Ziad Kobti, Professor and Director of
> the School of Computer Science,
> University of Windsor, Ontario, Canada

Introduction

*"Education is the most powerful weapon
which you can use to change the world."*
~~ Nelson Mandela

Is there indeed a "secret" to achieving all-round success in college and university? Why are some people A-students while others aren't? To even complicate this idea, one can ask – how come some students hold part-time jobs while enrolled in full-time course workload, and yet they ace their courses? What about students who graduate with GPA of 3.0 or 3.5 out of 4? How did they manage to pull that through? As if all of this is not enough, some students receive job offers even before their graduation. How on earth do they do it? These and many more similar questions may have crossed your mind at specific points.

You may have wondered if you can accomplish such remarkable feats. "Yes, you can!" A straightforward way to prove this is to remind you that thousands, possibly millions, of students have done it. If you give yourself enough time to reflect, I bet you will find that you know one or two students like that. If they can do it, you can too.

In pursuit of academic excellence

A person's background and early experiences may affect how that person approaches life, studies, and excellence. For example, all through my education - from primary to secondary to university – I had always wondered what separated high achievers from the average or low achieving students, having observed and admired high-performing students. Upon reflection, I suppose that was one of the reasons I was able to excel at school. In the summer of 2015, I completed a BSc program in Computer Science with specialization in Software Engineering at the University of Windsor, Ontario, Canada. I graduated summa cum laude (great distinction) reserved for students graduating with GPA of 3.6+ out of 4.

Students, who are focused on achieving success, will apply themselves entirely to their studies, to the extent that they would earn awards that might even come with financial benefits. It is impressive to aim for excellence and to achieve many by-products in the process. For example, during the course of my studying at university, I received some honours and recognitions including the Golden Key International Honour Society membership, which is awarded to the top 15% in a program; the Dean's Honour Roll List and Outstanding Scholar Awards, which are awarded to students with a GPA equivalent of at least 3.6 out of 4. Interestingly, I earned these awards for each academic year I completed. In addition, I also earned an Outstanding Performance in Co-operative Education (co-op) Work 2014.

What is worthy to note, is that in spite of all these achievements and recognition, I still had several challenges. There were times I experienced such "low times" that I had to agree with the popular maxim that on the road to success there are curves of failures. However, instead of this to discourage a focused student, it could actually serve as further inspiration. Why do I say this? If students realize that every success is accompanied by several attempts and several challenging opportunities, then they can be energized to find the tenacity and strength to continue pushing through every obstacle when obstacles present themselves.

The need to maintain a balanced school life

A successful student who is focused on achieving excellence will also aspire to have a balanced social life. Outside of academia, there are other activities, which help to provide a well-rounded, successful student. Therefore, endeavouring to incorporate extracurricular activities becomes very important. As a high achieving student, I too was involved in extracurricular activities. Some sources have preferred to call it "co-curricular activities" because they do help to further learning at a different dimension and in a different way. For example, I was involved in several extracurricular activities on campus, including participating in mentorship programs, for 3 and a half out of the 5 years I was at university. In this capacity, I had the opportunity to work with students to create goals, to develop a plan to achieve those goals and then encourage them to follow through with executing the plans pertaining to the goals.

As much as possible, I encourage students to set goals across the spectrum, encompassing academic, social and personal goals. In addition to serving as a mentor, I also served as the leader of the ushering department at the church I attended, for about 2 out of the 5 years I was at university. I was also the Vice President of the church youth group, for about a year and a half, and I was involved with other programs and activities in the church. Added to this, is another 15 months of real work world experience in my field, software engineering, through my participation in the co-op program. A combination of these activities not only helps to broaden a student's perspectives, but it also helps them acquire leadership, negotiation and time management skills among other valuable soft skills which are valuable in the world of work.

Ok! Please understand that I had shared my success stories not to brag or blow my trumpet. I only want to show you that you can achieve any goals you set for yourself in the areas of your life that matter to you – academic, spiritual, physical, mental, and so forth. That is basically what all-round success is all about, and that is what you will learn as you peruse the pages of this book. Moreover, with the level of technological advancement in this era, you have at your fingertips the information and resources needed to accomplish your goals. I, therefore, urge you to make full use of these opportunities, while you can.

Diligence, self-discipline and commitment are required

According to Andrew Carnegie, "Anything worth having in life is worth working for." Throughout history, it is difficult (and perhaps impossible) to find one person who didn't work hard to achieve what he or she had desired. Likewise, if you must fulfill your desires, goals, objectives (in the areas of academic, physical, spiritual, or mental), you must be diligent. It takes self-discipline to develop successful habits and commitment to keep up with those habits. Good habits - such as maintaining daily, weekly, and semester schedules, managing your time correctly, and nursing a positive mental attitude
– can make the difference between an A-student and the other students; they can also determine whether or not you'll achieve your goals.

Who is this book written for?

If you are a high school student warming up to enroll in university or college; or you are currently living the university or college life, then this book is for you. If you are happy with your current academic performance or you are beating yourself up about it, longing for better grades, this book is for you. Are you struggling to balance academic work with extracurricular or mental activities? If any of those captured your current state then you are holding the right book. This book won't only help you achieve the academic success you desire, but it will also guide you on how to excel outside the academic realm so that you can make the most of the time you'll spend at the post-secondary school of your choice and achieve the all-round success you desire.

How this book is organized

This book is divided into three parts which are arranged in a logical order.

1. Part 1, "On your marks, set – the preparation," will provide you will tasty nuggets you can use to start off your school career journey in the best way possible. The ideas cover areas such as the Big 5s (critical for having a solid beginning), choosing a school and a program of study, and picking the right courses to take. You'll learn why it is essential to practice the process of idealization before you start out on this journey, and what factors you should consider when selecting a school and a major.

2. Part 2, "Go - in motion," will supply you with tips and guidelines required to have a strong start, set SMART goals, maximize your time using "life-saving" scheduling tools, and maintain a balanced life. You will also get some insights into how to study effectively like an A-student, write excellent papers, make compelling presentations, and ace your exams.

3. Part 3, "Approaching the finish line"; here you'll learn how to complete your school journey just as strong as you had begun. Besides, you'll also learn how to position yourself for the next phase of life, after you graduate. Be it pursuing a post-graduate degree or securing a dream job.

How to get the most from this book

Reading a book like this one isn't meant just to increase your wealth of knowledge alone but to change the state of your mind and spur you to action. For this reason, you'll be greeted with a "Roll up your sleeves" section at the end of each chapter. The section has a couple of action exercises prepared for you to practice what was covered in each chapter. If you can, write down your responses to the questions somewhere you can always refer to, for example, in a diary, or on sticky notes which you can stick to a wall in your room. Getting involved with the action exercises is undoubtedly a great way to learn, and Benjamin Franklin attests to that when he said, "Tell me, and I forget, teach me, and I remember, involve me, and I learn."

Endeavour to remember this one thing: nobody is smarter or better than you per se; he or she just knows something you don't yet know or does something you don't yet do or have not yet decided to do. I believe that if you purposefully engage with this book, you'll learn, the secret of how to maximize time spent pursuing post-secondary education and eventually achieve the all-round success that you so desire. You too can become an example to cite when people are trying to encourage others.

On that note, I would like to congratulate you on the decision to further your education. See you in the pages ahead!

Part 1

"On your marks! Set!"
- The preparation

CHAPTER ONE

Begin with the end in mind

*"Begin with the end in mind. Start with the
end outcome then work backwards to
make your dreams possible."*
~~ Wayne D. Dyer

Have you ever embarked on an adventurous journey, say, to a distant, unfamiliar place? Or lately, have you visited an amusement park outside your city, whether with friends and family or alone? If you've been in any of those situations, you'll agree with me that proper planning is really critical to the success of those outings. For the adventurous journey, for example, you probably had to determine beforehand: whom you'll travel with (fun-filled and positive-minded individuals will be the best), what you plan to do during the trip and at the final destination, and possibly, how you'd conduct yourself in the unfamiliar place. In essence, you had orchestrated a mental play of the adventure before jumping out to live the play in reality.

Just as you would plan for an adventurous trip to an unfamiliar place, you would want to do the same before you start out on your college or university journey. A plan (let's call it a "school life plan," shall we?), which will serve as a map, has to be in place to help you navigate the maze of your post-secondary school journey all through till the desired end.

In this chapter, I'll walk you through the Big 5s, which are vital questions you'll need to consider as you get started on the journey (as a way of building the "school life plan"). You'll also see why those questions are essential to your success in school.

The Big 5s: the school life plan

The Big 5s are basically five questions which you want to answer and run with to enable you to achieve the all-round success that you desire.

1. Why am I pursuing a post-secondary degree?

Before taking any action, it always helps to ask the question, "why?" In your case, at this moment, the question can be phrased as "why am I going to college?" Or "why am I going to university?" The more sincerely and accurately you can answer this question, the more you'll get out from your experience at the school of your choice. Some answers students usually give to this question include:

● To acquire the knowledge and skills required to become a professional in my field of interest,
● To please my parents,
● To make new friends,
● To develop a sense of independence and responsibility,
● To have fun, and so on.

Irrespective of the reasons other students may have presented, just be sure that you are genuinely convinced about the reasons you choose; that they are authentic to you. Those reasons will eventually become part of the building blocks of motivation for you as you advance on this journey.

3

2. What kind of "school life" do I plan to adopt?

I have heard people say different interesting things about post-secondary institutions, i.e. college and university. For example, "that is where you discover who you truly are" or "that is where you meet your greatest fears." Irrespective of whether those are true or not, I want you to know that you can choose for yourself what you want your school life to be. But then you can either live the school life you plan for yourself, or you drift around living a life drafted by others. If you end up drifting around and living a life drafted by others, I can assure you that the end result will not be favourable.

A friend of mine, who went to the same university as I did, once shared the story of her roommate while she was still in her first year. Her roommate was wanton and lived a somewhat loose life on campus, indulging excessively in orgies and other harmful activities. It wasn't long before she contracted a venereal disease and unfortunately lost her life before completing her program. It is an unfortunate story - I know. And, I didn't give that example to sadden you, but to only let you know how impactful the choices you make about your school life can be to your overall journey.

So, the beginning is an excellent time to determine the [safe] lifestyle you plan to live on campus. Then, purpose in your heart to follow it through, and you won't be sorry at the end - I promise you.

3. What kind of activities will I get involved in and which ones do I dare not do?

The activities you spend most your time doing may determine how people perceive you and possibly what names you may be dubbed. If you are found in just about every house party

4

organized around campus, you may be tagged a party-goer; if you are in the library 24/7; you'll likely be nicknamed the librarian or an egghead; probably you'll be called a glutton if you are always found munching in the cafeteria. Whether people call you names or not isn't really the crux of this point at all. The main thing here is to ensure that the activities you mostly partake in, are in alignment with your overall goals. In other words, you need to decide whether or not the results of activity will move you towards achieving your goal or not. If it does, go for it, and if it does not, you may want to consider avoiding it.

For example, before getting started with my university program, I remember how fascinated I felt just reading about the various resources available at the university of my choice. The Math and Statistics Lab, the Computer Science Commons, the gym, the library, amongst the others - were places I knew I'd hang around most of the time. For you, it may be that you are interested in music or sports or drama. In that case, you may anticipate getting involved in activities that revolve around those areas. Once you've identified those activities that'll move you in the direction of your goal, you're able to detect and keep away from those that won't. This is very important if you want to succeed and enjoy the journey on the way to success.

4. What kind of friends will I associate with?

Chaplain Ronnie Melancon once remarked, "Show me your friends and I'll show you your future." Surely, you have heard that saying or a similar one countless times; I can't overemphasize how true and real it is. There are numerous stories about good students, who upon enrolling in a college or university, got negatively influenced by some bad students and ended up derailed. In most cases, the end never was happy especially for the used-to-be good students. On the other hand, there are many stories of good folks who met with other good folks and then merged forces to achieve a more fruitful experience (I bet that is what you want). At school, you'll encounter a very wide range of people and personalities: the good, the bad, the cool, the not-too-cool, and many more. It is your responsibility to choose those you'll continuously hang around with and those whom you won't allow into your space. I am hoping that you'll choose your friends wisely because your friends can either propel you to achieve your end goals or impede you from getting there.

5. **What kind of legacy do I plan to leave behind after I graduate?**
    Whether you're aware of it or not, you'll be leaving a legacy behind upon your graduation from school. So, you need to answer the question – "What do I want to be remembered for?"

    Trust me; this is the best time to start thinking about this question - right before you begin your school journey. Doing this will motivate you to begin this journey with its end in mind. Note also that your legacy may either be good or bad. You can choose to be known as that guy who partied and gave himself to drinking, or that girl who lived a loose and reckless life, or that fellow who always stole the show at awards ceremonies, or that dude who always argued and fought with everyone during lectures. I believe you'll feel fulfilled when, few years after your graduation, you look back and have no regrets about the legacy you had established at your school.

    By earnestly answering these questions (and other questions that may be triggered by these ones), I believe that you'll be on the way to mapping out a solid school life plan, which you can rely on as you navigate this important journey.

The Value of the Big 5s
You may be questioning the rationale behind the Big 5s. But before

you entirely dismiss this idea, let me give you some reasons why you should consider it:

1. **It will help you focus on your goal and avoid drifting:**
   You may have heard the saying that, "Failure to plan is equivalent to planning to fail." Planning, as you know is a crucial part of any venture as without it, the chances of failure are high. When you take the time to create and imagine the experiences you desire and determine your priorities and friends, you'll be more focused as you strive to achieve your goals and objectives. Students who fail to take this exercise seldom reach the desired end because in the first place none was established; such students will only drift and go anywhere the wind blows. You surely don't want that happening to you.

2. **It will motivate you and fortify your commitment to yourself:**
   As humans, there is a tendency for us to lose our driving force and zeal halfway along a long journey irrespective of how important that journey may be. In times like that, the only way we can plunge ahead is to recall the commitments and objectives we had established before the journey. Regarding your post-secondary education journey, creating a school life plan (the Big 5s) will serve as your commitment which will motivate you especially when things get tough.

3. **It eases decision making:**
   Answering the Big 5s will give you a clear picture of your dos and don'ts. Those, of course, will help you reach decisions quickly and ensure that you have little or no regrets later on. For instance, suppose you had committed to abstaining from harmful activities such as smoking, orgies and excessive drinking, but then some associates who indulge in those acts invite you to join them. If a commitment is genuinely what it

should be, then you won't think twice before responding to them with, "No thanks - I am the wrong folk to ask." On the other hand, having planned to ace your exams, you'll probably respond positively to industrious friends who beckon on you to brainstorm and study together. Your commitment, the responses to those 5 questions, is what will give you the willpower to respond in this manner. Without it, you'll likely give in to temptations or miss out on opportunities.

Students who responded honestly and appropriately to those 5 questions (and similar ones) have been known to attribute their success in school to their responses. The anecdotal evidence has thus led me to firmly believe that the exercise will work wonders for you as well. I invite you to give some thoughts to the Big 5s and to present your own responses. It will also help if you can write these down in a notebook which you can refer to from time to time.

How the Big 5s can help you
I have asked a friend of mine Paul Awede to share his story based off of the Big 5s [that make up the school life plan]. Just so you know, during his undergrad, Paul graduated with a first-class in Computer Engineering from Queen's University, Ontario, Canada. In fact, at the time of writing, he is currently a project manager at a reputable IT company, and he is advancing well in his career.

Here is a synopsis of his response to the Big 5s:
Firstly, deciding whether to pursue a post-secondary degree or not, is a major decision. Personally speaking, my main reason was the thought of getting a lucrative job after the completion of my degree. I also told myself that I needed to get excellent grades, in order to get a lucrative job. This motivated me to study hard, and not allow any distractions to derail me from achieving my goal.

Always remind yourself the reason why you are pursuing your degree, because the right reasons will help you when the going gets tough.

Secondly, if you've seen the movie "Lion King", you probably remember the conversation between Mufasa and Simba around the time Simba seemed to have forgotten who he was. "Remember who you are" is a phrase you should not forget. It doesn't matter where in the world you find yourself, your moral values and beliefs should not be thrown away especially when you get into University.

Thirdly, it is essential to get involved in activities that will help you achieve your ultimate goal of finishing well, those activities that align with your values and beliefs.

Fourthly, it is critical to associate with like-minded friends. If the friends you hang out with don't add value to your life, you should reconsider your friendship with them. At various stages of your university life, you'll require advice, help, and assistance; so it is essential to have the right kind of people around you at such times (if not at all times).

Finally, it is actually left to you to decide on the legacy you plan to leave behind. Remember we are a product of our decisions, not a product of our circumstances. Every little act of kindness you show goes a long way. Though you might forget about it, the recipients of your good deeds won't forget. In any case, it is a good thing to be dedicated to your school work, and be the best you can possibly be, whether people notice or not. These are precious questions, and I believe so firmly, that by paying attention to them, you'll be positioning yourself to achieve the success you desire. Goodluck!

In the next chapter, you'll gain insight into how to select the right program of study and courses as well as the right school.

Roll up your sleeves

Spend some time to think about the following:

1. Why are you pursuing a post-secondary education?
2. What kind of lifestyle do you plan to adopt at school?
3. What kind of activities will you indulge in and which ones will you flee from?
4. What kind of friends will you choose to associate with? What values will they add to you and what will you contribute to their lives?
5. What do you want to be remembered for after you graduate?

CHAPTER TWO

The major, the school, and the courses; get them right

"When you know what you want, and
want it bad enough, you will find a way
to get it."
~~ Jim Rohn

When was the last time you ordered a meal from a restaurant or ate out? I can probably describe the entire ordering process that took place starting from what may have occurred inside your mind.

First of all, you had to decide what food exactly you wanted to munch; maybe it was pizza, burger, exotic cake, bagel and hot chocolate (the breakfast combo), or fried rice with chicken. The next step you took was to determine which fast food restaurant did the best job at preparing the food you had selected and, if you were in a good mood, you didn't overthink about the cost (hopefully you aren't always in that mood). So, for example, suppose you felt like eating crispy fried chicken, you probably ordered it from Kentucky Fried Chicken (KFC). Or perhaps, you tended toward Domino's Pizza if you desired pizza. You probably won't visit KFC if you hungered for pizza - would you? So, basically in those instances, you had first to identify what food precisely you desired before going ahead to choose the best place where you can obtain it, given your available resources.

The same principle can be applied when choosing a major (or program of studies, as some call it) and a post-secondary institution. It is befitting that you figure out first what program you want to enrol in and that will help you choose the right post-secondary institution. In fact, William J. Bennett, the secretary of education under President Reagan of the United States, said it best when he affirmed that, "a four-year college program is worth it for students who take the right subject at the right place for the right price."[1] That tells you how important it is to choose a course of study before deciding what college or university to enroll in.

Following this sequence will definitely help you quickly narrow down your options and guide you toward arriving at a decision in reasonable time. Obviously, this may not be the only way, but it is one way that works. The truth is that certain universities or colleges may not offer the program(s) of your choice; so having this knowledge will help you decide which schools to discard from your exploration list.

In this chapter, I'll walk you through key factors that will guide you toward selecting the right major, the right school and the right courses. That said, let us dive straight into considerations to look out for when choosing a major.

Selecting the right major

I must say, in all honesty, that choosing a major isn't as easy as ordering your favourite food. At least I can say this from my own experience. I remember while I was trying to finish secondary school I had struggled with choosing a major for post-secondary phase even though at that time some of my friends seemed confident about what they wanted. But as time went on, I soon discovered what major was right for me.

If you find yourself in that situation where you lack regarding your major, worry no more, because by the end of this chapter you should have some ideas about what you want to study (of course, provided that you do the required exercises).

The following will serve as a guide:

1. Identify your strengths and passions:

Looking at the courses you are currently taking at your secondary or high school: which are you passionate about and most interested in? Which do you do well at and also ace almost with ease? Which do you perform poorly at and bomb badly? I believe this is a perfect place to start. If you are the kind who can't stand working with numbers, "dy/dx" and other advanced mathematics topics, then it may not be a good idea to choose mathematics or core engineering programs. Also, suppose you find it boring reading articles, journals or research papers, and you know that writing isn't your thing, it probably isn't ideal to pursue a degree in English or Literature or History. These are just a few examples, but I hope you get the idea. The bottom line is for you to choose a program that you are good at and interested in (you can tell this by the core courses that make up the program).

Of course, you may challenge yourself and declare, for example, "I want to turn this area of weakness to an area of strength," so you pick a major you aren't interested in or one that you are not fundamentally strong at. No one will stop you from doing this so long as you know what you are doing and that this action agrees with your goals. The reason you should consider your passion and interest when choosing a major is that, as you progress in your study, the journey gets tougher and tougher, and with no interest and passion, you'll likely yield to the pressure and give up halfway. I know of a lot of people who started with one major, but at the first appearance of a fierce challenge, they quit and began looking for another major (possibly because they lacked interest from the start).

Your strengths and passions will tell you what options to consider whereas your weaknesses will yell which ones to flee from and ignore.

2. Recall your future ambition (or career) and dream:

Imagining the future has always proved useful in making critical decisions in life and here is one example where that applies. In choosing your major, you also need to answer the questions: "What do I see myself doing in the future?" "What are my dreams and ambitions?" Maybe you have always dreamt of becoming an entrepreneur or a doctor then you may consider taking a program in Business or Medicine respectively.

Before he got admitted into the university, my brother, Daniel was always sure about what he dreamt of becoming when he grew up. Whenever he was asked what he wanted to become in the future, "a doctor," he would respond almost instantly. No wonder it wasn't a hassle for him choosing a major at university. He is currently in his 3rd year studying Medicine, and I am very proud of his excellent performance thus far (the guy actually receives awards every academic year).

Just to be clear on this point, your career dream isn't the only factor that will determine what major to choose. It is essential to have an idea of what your career ambition is so that you don't go off course when picking a major. There are individuals who, for example, took up a major in physics and became software developers (probably because of their strong Maths background and exposure to programming). However, you can't pick up a major in music when you plan on becoming a dentist in the future (I don't see how that will work).

3. Consider the next phase:

Going to university is not an end in itself, but it's a means to an end. After you complete your program, I suppose the next step is to get a lucrative job (at least that is the ambition for the majority; you'll be eager to get back the money you spent on tuition fees and the rest). Probably another logical step will be to pursue advanced studies or start up a business

To this end, you'll have to answer the question: "What program will increase my chances of advancing in the next phase?" This will be very important if you plan to secure a job immediately after completing your undergrad program. If, on the other hand, you plan to further your undergrad study by enrolling for a Master's or Ph.D. program, then you have to choose a program that will prepare you for that next phase. Also, in the event that you plan to start up your own business after you graduate (which is a great idea), you have to decide which program will help you acquire the skills required for you to succeed in the business you have in mind.

You don't have to beat yourself down if you don't know for sure what the next phase is, but, knowing it will help you make decisions promptly. As much as you can, try to think and plan ahead and you'll develop a beneficial habit.

4. Seek counsel:

If you need help in choosing a major, don't hesitate to meet with an academic adviser. The advisers are always there to guide you. In some cases, it helps to consult with an adviser with whom you can relate well since you are likely to benefit most from such person.

Don't be discouraged if you are unable to decide on a major right away. These points are more like food for thought, and I am hoping you'll spend the time to ponder over them till you get what you're looking for. Now that you have an idea of the "What," let us focus on the "Where."

Selecting the right post-secondary institution

I am hoping that you have an idea of what major you plan to pursue (the "What"); so now, we can delve into some key factors to consider when selecting a post-secondary institution.

Generally, once you have decided that you want to undertake post-secondary education, you need to consider the following:

1. Admission requirements:

The only way you can get admitted into a school is if you meet its admission requirements. The admission requirements usually come in two parts: one, the country requirement which applies to international students; two, the program requirement which applies to both domestic and international students.

Generally speaking, schools will demand a standard qualification based on your nationality or the country from where you completed your secondary education. Some examples of such country requirement include USA Senior High School for Americans (folks from USA), West African Senior School Certificate results (WASSCE) for Nigerians, Diploma di Maturita Magistrale (Secondary School Certificate) for Italians, Senior High School Graduation Diploma and Chinese university entrance examination (NCEE Gao Kao) for Chinese, and so forth.

On the other hand, the program requirement specifies the core subjects which you ought to have completed at your high school or secondary school to be considered for a particular major. For example, the program requirement for an undergraduate program in Physics could include the following: Grade 12 Mathematics and Physics; likewise, for a Mechanical Engineering program, the requirement could include Mathematics, Physics and Chemistry. A minimum score or cutoff mark may be included with the program requirement. In addition to those courses, a Language Proficiency Test will likely be required for students whose first language is different from the language of instruction at the school. For example, if your first language is Greek or Cantonese and you are enrolling in a school in the United States or

Canada where English is the language of instruction, then you'll be required to write an English Language Proficiency Test.

This information about the admission requirements should be readily available to you on the school's website. Being aware of the availability of such information, it is a good idea for you to look out for these requirements, especially the program requirements, well in advance of you applying, so you can work hard enough to meet them.

2. Program availability:

Not all schools will offer the program you want. It has been observed that schools tend to focus on specific fields for which they are well-known for excellence when compared to other schools. So, once you are sure about the program you plan to pursue, you can then filter out from your list those schools that don't offer such program.

3. Reputation and Cost:

I am sure while undertaking your school hunt; you probably had to google top universities or colleges offering a particular program. It is almost instinctive to consider the most reputable brands before making a decision. Getting a degree from Oxford, Harvard or Cambridge will be truly remarkable and will open doors for you. However, the big question is – can you afford the cost? If yes, sure - go for it! But if you can't, that's fine. This is the time to remember the proverb, "Cut your coat according to your size." Find a school you can afford. After all, one who enrolls in a highly reputable school but fails to maximize the opportunity is no better off someone else who couldn't afford such a high privilege yet maximally utilizes what he or she could pay for.

In the end, what really matters most is whether you applied yourself and made the best of what you could afford.

4. Location:

The location of the school you choose will play a key role in determining whether you will live on-campus, off-campus or at home with your family. Each option has its own pros and cons which should be weighed.

Staying on-campus will suit students who live very far away from school and have nowhere around the school area to stay. For example, international students, whose homes are thousands of miles away, will benefit more from this option. Besides that, staying on-campus gives students ready access to the school facilities such as the library, labs, gym, etc. However, students who live on-campus and are away from their homes will miss the comfort of their family and frequently suffer from homesickness (I can't deny this one).In addition, the cost of living on-campus may not be friendly compared to the other options. But it's usually a good option for freshmen/freshwomen who are international students.

Living off-campus isn't a bad idea. You can rent a house along with your friends or secure a single room and live with strangers. Interestingly, this could be an excellent avenue to make new friends. Another possibility is renting a condominium where you can live a very comfortable life. Depending on the distance from school to the off-campus residence, you can still easily access the school facilities but perhaps not as readily as those living on-campus. With this option, you can claim to live in "your own house," cook whatever you want, live with whomever you choose and do just about anything in your house (so long as the real homeowner is ok with it, of course). One downside here is that the activities of your housemates may distract and discomfort you.

However, with house rules in place, as expected, this should not be too much of an issue.

Last but not the least, you can consider living in the family house. This option is desirable by most students. Here you remain under the same roof with your lovely family, eating your mom's delicious meals (or your dad's, whoever the better cook is) and enjoying the company of your siblings or neighbourhood homies. Also, you won't have to worry about rent, parking, utilities and the rest. However, transporting yourself to school may be a hassle especially if your family house is far from your school. On top of that, access to school facilities may prove to be a problem especially if you are the kind who can't study at home, for example.

Whatever the case, you have to work things out with your parents/guardians to see which option suits you best.

When registering for courses

Here are some essential tips to consider when registering for courses in a semester:

1. Learn about available courses:

It is always a good idea to visit the course catalogue available on the school's student portal (you need to familiarize yourself with this resource). From the student portal, you can learn about the different courses offered in a given semester and possibly for an academic year. For each course, you can find out about: the course description, the required textbook(s), the professor teaching the course, the lecture hours and location, and other relevant course-related information. With good knowledge of all these, you'll be well-informed to make wise decisions about the courses to take.

2. Register early:

Enrolment in courses at most schools is usually on the basis of first-come-first-serve. So, if you really want to get into the best lecture sections (late morning and early afternoon) as opposed to odd hours (say 8:30 am or 7pm), you just have to register early. Stay attentive and always watch out for when the flag goes down for course registration to begin.

3. Select courses that fulfill your degree requirements:

Most schools offer a wide range of courses, and so it is easy to get lost when it's time to register for courses. For this reason, ensure that the courses you pick actually count toward the fulfillment of your degree requirements. You can verify this by either referring to the degree audit (a tool that tracks your progress towards the completion of your degree and recommends courses as well), if available to you or by inquiring from an academic adviser. Remember you won't be eligible to graduate until you complete all the required courses associated with your degree requirements.

4. Consider taking elective courses:

It can be boring to take only courses that are related to your major. Besides that, one of the reasons for enrolling in post-secondary education is to expand your horizons, and one way to do that is to take elective courses (that is courses that are unrelated to your major but can count towards the completion of your degree). For example, at the university I attended, the Computer Science Honors program requires that students choose elective courses from fields such as psychology, biology, philosophy, sociology, media and communication, art and language, astrology, economics, business, accounting, and so forth. That is how even as a computer science major, I ended up taking courses in psychology, business, communications, and a couple other unrelated fields. Indeed, the knowledge and skills I acquired by taking those courses really did me a lot of good and continue to serve me well, even now that I have graduated and am gainfully employed in my profession.

5. **Balance your course load:**

For your course load, each semester, endeavour to create a right mix of heavy and light courses (that is, if you have the choice). It can be unbearable if all of your courses in a particular semester are crushing you down, and there is no course to run to for a break. One good idea is to try a combination of lightweight elective courses and heavyweight major courses. Just don't combine heavyweight elective courses with heavyweight major courses or else get ready for a knockout.

6. **Space out your lecture times:**

Depending on how many lectures you'll have each day, you should think about the time frame between each lecture. If you can, try to choose lecture hours such that you'll have some time between your lectures. You'll need some time to, at least, make it early to the next lecture and possibly to quickly review your lecture notes. Arriving late to lectures is usually not fun.

7. **Pay attention to pre- and co-requisite courses:**

Before you can take certain courses, you may need to prove that you've completed a specific course (called a prerequisite course). Also, in order to register for specific courses, you may be required to register for another course at the same time (a co-requisite course is what this one is called). Watch out for these two types of courses and plan your course load correctly, so you don't miss a required course in a semester because you don't have the prerequisite course(s) completed.

8. Don't avoid the lab:

For specific fields such as science, math, media and communication, and amongst many others – there is usually a lab section which is to be taken together with the lecture in a given semester. You are strongly advised to enroll in a lab section if it is part of a course you plan to take. Think about it this way: the lecture is more of the theory side and the lab the practical side of the course; you need both sides to enjoy the full benefits of such courses that offer both lecture and lab.

Another reason you want to partake in the lab is that you'll gain deeper understanding and insight into concepts taught during the lectures. Whether it is solving problems on differential equations in a Vector Calculus course or experimenting with acids and base in a Chemistry course, participating in the lab will undoubtedly help deepen your understanding of critical concepts. One more thing: assignments in the lab can appear in tests and exams, so take the lab seriously.

9. Stuck? Get help immediately:

As usual, if you encounter any difficulty registering for courses, don't hesitate to consult an academic adviser. For upper-year students (those in 3rd year or above), consider meeting with a faculty adviser in your department instead of a general academic adviser. The former will have more specific and in-depth responses especially regarding your major compared to the latter.

Why you shouldn't choose that course or major

I feel so strongly that this chapter won't be complete without me discussing why you shouldn't pick a particular major or course. You have seen some factors to consider when choosing a major and a school. To crown it up, there are a couple of reasons why you shouldn't select a major or course. They include:

1. "All my friends selected it":

This is not uncommon so you should watch out for this one. Most times people get caught up in the bandwagon effect and blindly follow the crowd. It is good sometimes (of course, only when it yields a positive outcome), but other times it can be an ordeal. Someone I know once shared with me the story of his experience as a fresher at university. Having got admission into a university (with a couple of his friends), he had selected a program in the Sciences only because his friends did the same. His friends performed outstandingly well in their majors because they not only had a passion for the major and the required courses, but they also had a knack for the Sciences in general. On the other hand, my friend not only struggled with the program but was literally at the bottom of the class while his friends were way ahead of him. While he remained at the same academic level, repeating several courses, his friends advanced to the next academic level as they soon abandoned him. It was after some profound reflections that he followed his heart and enrolled in a program at which he excelled. Sadly, he had already spent a year or two drifting from coast to coast and had made no progress in his study, but thank God he later ended well.

The lesson here is straightforward: your friends shouldn't choose major or courses for you – be in charge and choose for yourself.

2. "It is a piece of cake":

While it is clear that good grades are always desirable by all, care must be taken to ensure that they aren't obtained at the expense of your personal growth and development. What I mean here is that you can't merely enroll in a course because you only plan to boost your GPA (Grade Point Average). You also need to think of the values the courses you plan to take will add to you and what skills you'll acquire by taking the courses. Because at the end of it all, it isn't so much about how high your GPA is, but about how much skills and values you have gained.

In today's job market, most employers, when making hiring decisions, tend to focus more on skills and core values than on school grades. You may take only easy courses throughout your school year and obtain high scores, but you'll never challenge yourself enough to maximize your potentials fully. At your post-secondary institution, you'll have the opportunity to choose courses that will broaden your horizon and teach you skills that will help your overall improvement.

In short, I guess the summary here is to try to maintain a right balance between learning and obtaining great grades (one mustn't be favoured over and above the other).

3. "Others will think I am smart":

This is one of the greatest mistakes any student will ever make: enrolling in a major or taking a course just so people can think highly of him or her. I think the first thing to remember is that you are pursuing a degree for yourself and not for anyone else. The certificate of completion you'll receive upon graduation will be inscribed with your name and no one else's. It is about your true success and not some fake one.

Also, don't take hard courses merely to prove to yourself or to others that you are smart – you won't be doing yourself any good at the end of the day especially if your performance is terrible. Stick to your desired major and to the required courses – they are already challenging enough so why give yourself more pressure?

Hopefully, by now, you know how to go about figuring out your major, your school and your courses. Like I mentioned earlier, this step may not be as easy as ordering your choice food from a restaurant, but it is a worthy step to take. I believe somewhere along your school journey you'll be glad you considered these points. The way you begin a journey to a reasonable degree can affect the quality of the journey, at least during the early phases. In the next chapter, I'll provide you with useful tips that give you the boost you require to create a compelling start on your academic career journey.

Roll up your sleeves

1. Have you selected a major yet? If not, take a stab at the following questions and let them guide you:
   a. Considering your secondary school courses, which courses are you passionate about and interested in? Which do you do well at and "ace" with ease?
   b. What do you see yourself doing in the future? What are your dreams and ambitions?
   c. What major will increase your chances of reaching your next life phase (i.e. landing a lucrative job or pursuing a graduate program or starting a business)?

2. Have you made up your mind yet on the university or college you'll like to attend? If not, let the following factors be your guide when considering different schools:
   a. Admission requirement: Have you met the admission requirement for the school?
   b. Program availability: Does the school offer the major you intend to pursue?
   c. Reputation: Does the school possess solid reputation and facilities for the field you have in mind?
   d. Cost: Can you afford the tuition fees for the school?
   e. Location: If you get admitted to the school, where will you live - on campus or off campus?

3. It is vital that you choose your courses carefully. Refer to the points in the "When registering for courses" section when picking your courses.

4. Resolve that you'll not choose a major or enroll in a course for any of the following reasons:
   a. "All my friends selected it"
   b. "It is a piece of cake."
   c. "Others will think I am smart." journey all through till the desired end.

Part 2
"Go!" - In motion"

CHAPTER THREE

Start strong, start well

"A good start is half the battle."
~~ Plato

In the journey of your academic career, having a good start is critical as it can determine how well and quickly you complete the journey. The earlier you know about specific success secrets [for a good start] and begin applying them, the earlier you'll begin noticing satisfying results. This section is meant to equip you with a number of those good-start success secrets. In this chapter, I'll share with you the benefits of attending orientation sessions, various resources on campus and how to maximize them, how to get the best from lectures, and how to put these all together to become a highly effective student. Commit to these, and you'll be golden.

The arrival

(This subtopic - "The arrival" - was intended for students who'll be living on the campus residence. If this doesn't apply to you, please feel free to move on to the next subtopic - "Don't miss orientations.")

It is a beautiful sunny day. You touch down from a car driven by a family member, a friend or maybe even a cab driver. The car trunk jerks open and your luggage is presented to you. Saying goodbye to the person who gave you a ride, perhaps with tears streaming down your eyes, you begin pondering on how quickly this day came by (or maybe you are happy). The car engine starts off, the car disappears from your sight and you are left alone with your luggage. You brace yourself, and with a feeling of doubt mixed with excitement, you begin to ask yourself - "Where do I go from here?"

This is a typical first-time arrival experience for many fresh students who arrive on campus especially for those who will be staying on the campus residence. It is vital for you to know that schools are continually working hard to ensure that this arrival experience for students, especially international students, is as smooth and pleasant as can be. For example, some schools have set up a soft landing program were international students who arrive into the country during operation hours get picked up from the airport and then transported to the school campus. However, those who arrive outside operation hours get to lodge into a hotel till the next day when they can make their way to the campus. If you are an international student, find out if such program exists at your school. If it does, be sure to take advantage of it.

As you step on the school's soil, if you have chosen to live on-campus, you should locate the residence services on campus to obtain information about your resident building and room so you can unpack and move freely. For international students, a must-visit place is the International Student Office where you'll be welcomed warmly to your new home away from home and be filled in on very important matters such as obtaining advice on academic and immigration issues, opening a bank account, getting around on campus, amongst many others. Information on obtaining your student card, setting up your school email account, attending orientations (strongly recommended), navigating campus, should communicated to you by the school management.

Don't sweat it at all. This is one of the most exciting periods, as you'll encounter novel scenes and people.

Don't miss orientations

As they say, "When you are in Rome, act like the Romans." Being new to a school environment and perhaps a country, especially if you are an international student, it behooves you to get acclimatized to the cultures of both the school and the country so you can blend in easily. A great way to get started on this is by attending orientations. Personally, I can't overemphasize how beneficial orientations are. On top of that, studies have shown that students who participate in orientation programmes tend to adapt and settle quickly into campus and academic life.

Usually in the first month of resumption, there will be a couple of welcome and orientation occasions around campus organized by various faculties & departments (faculties as in Faculty of Law, Faculty of Science; departments as in School of Business, Languages & Arts departments, etc.), the International Student Associations, the students clubs & groups (for example, Engineers Without Borders, Golden Key International, etc), the Part-time Students Association, and so forth. You are strongly encouraged to attend whichever applies to you (it could even be more than one).

I remember vividly how my orientations turned out – very memorable. After settling on campus and completing the necessary check-in procedures, about a week later, I made it to the orientation organized for international students. At the event, I learnt about some of the cultural differences between my home country and the country where the university was situated. I also was intimated with the immigration requirements for international students, the demographics of the university, the myriad of resources and facilities available to students (See "How to make the most of the available resources on campus" Chapter 3 for more on this), and so many other useful information that I was glad to have known at that time. The event also featured a presentation by the international student academic adviser, at that time, who gave an overview of the academic system at the university. From that presentation, I was made aware of the workings of the grading system, the procedure to search for, register and drop courses, directions on using the student portal (it should be your tight buddy), and much other useful information. In general, the event was very insightful.

Besides that, I still remember my experience at a departmental orientation as a freshman at university, so vividly, it almost feels as if it was yesterday. After that orientation I thought to myself, "had I missed this event, I think I would have been screwed - big time!" As an international student, I was unable to complete registration for my courses while in my home country. Fortunately for me, at the departmental orientation, I was glad to have met with a faculty member who was also an academic adviser. This person was kind enough to assist me to register for courses that semester. In general, the event made me mentally and academically prepared for the journey ahead. As an added bonus, I even received a free, pretty t-shirt at the event, courtesy of the Faculty of Science.

Additionally, at both events, I made new friends, some of whom were citizens of my home country and others were in the same program as I was. The fascinating thing is that some of the friends I met at those events have become lifelong companions. I hope you have or have had, a splendid time at your orientations as well. Mostly, the goal is for you to get settled and prepared for the journey ahead. The earlier you get settled and know your way around the campus, the better it will be for you.

How to make the most of the available resources on campus

Achieving success in any endeavour requires not only that you work hard but equally that you understand and utilize the resources available to you. As mentioned earlier, orientation is a great way to learn about the various resources available to you on campus. By putting these resources to effective use, you'll significantly boost your chances of achieving the success you desire at school.

Having said that, here are some of those resources you should be sure to utilize:

1. Professors:

If you aren't used to being friends with your professors or instructors at school, then I urge you to turn a new leaf on that because professors are one of the most significant academic resource students can use. I say this based on my experience with my professors at my university. Actually, I had nursed a wrong preconception about professors, thinking them to be mean and brash people until I got to university where I realized how wrong I had thought.

During my undergrad days, I was known by the majority of the professors whose courses I had enrolled in, not for any reason but for my regular use of their office hours. Hardly was there a time when I approached them with questions or doubts related to their courses that they weren't able to answer me satisfactorily. In fact, professors are always happy to put students through difficulties, and they delight to see their students excel. Not only do professors know their stuff, but they also love what they do, having understood the truth that a candle loses nothing by lighting other candles. It is for this reason that a professor would put together review sessions outside lecture hours to prepare students for a tough assignment or an upcoming exam. It is also for the same reason that a professor would stay late after lecture hours to hold extra office hours, making himself or herself available to students.

Professors do this to ensure that students acquire all the useful knowledge required for them to succeed in their academic work. Thus, you'll be missing a lot if you don't leverage what they have to offer.

One specific area of which I highly recommend that you consult your professors is in seeking corrections or feedback on your assignments, tests or exams. So long as you didn't score a perfect on an exam, I think it is expedient that you meet with your professor to discuss what you did wrong. This is necessary to get you to become better prepared for any subsequent exams just so you don't make the same mistakes that will cost you some precious marks.

For example, suppose on your first midterm exam for Biology 101 you had scored 75% because you had lost all points allotted to 2 questions, out of 5 questions in total on that exam. Since most final exams tend to cover materials tested on both first and second midterm exams, there is a chance that those 2 questions which you failed to answer correctly on your first midterm exam will reappear, exactly or similarly, on the final exam. If that happens, you'll be toasted if you didn't already get corrections on those 2 questions before sitting for the final exam. Therefore, you endeavour to seek your professors for such corrections so you don't end up pulling your hairs, after it may have been too late.

Also, for your respective courses, take note of the office hours of your professors and utilize their office hours. You can almost be sure they will be glad to see you and work with you.

2. Teaching Assistants (TAs) & Graduate Assistants (GAs):

As much as they'd love to, professors can't always be available to help you out when needed, so they've arranged for Teaching Assistants, often referred to as "TAs" and/or Graduate Assistants "GAs," to stand in for them. TAs & GAs are students as well (TAs are usually undergrad students while the GAs are Masters or Ph.D. students), and they ought to have had an outstanding final grade on a course that's exactly or similar to the course which they are assisting the professors with. As a student, you may flow more freely with them as opposed to your professors especially if you are the kind of person who gets intimidated by authority figures. However, don't be too disappointed if, on some occasions, a TA or GA isn't able to help you out as expected; if or when that happens, seek help from other sources, remembering that TAs & GAs are students as well. Personally, during my undergrad, I benefited a lot from most of my TAs and GAs, and I am still friends with a few even until now.

As with your professors, find out the office hours of the TAs and GAs assigned to the courses you are enrolled in and endeavour to utilize their service.

3. Academic adviser:

If you ever need help searching for the right courses to take, register for or drop, don't hesitate to schedule an appointment with an academic adviser as soon as possible. Academic advisers have a long record of rescuing students from the heat of academic probation and the pain of withdrawal due to poor academic performance. In short, they don't only guide students on the best action steps to take regarding their academic work; they are also known to encourage students with firm words.

For instance, while pursuing my undergrad degree, the international student academic adviser at my university at that time, Mrs. Handsor, was a great source of encouragement to me. The signature text at the bottom of her emails always read - "People may forget what you said to them, but they will never forget how you made them feel." This should give you a glimpse of the kind of adviser she was. She had also been an academic adviser to her two kids who attended the same university where she had worked. According to her, she relates to students who sought her advice just as she would her own kids. She loved her role so dearly, and it shone through the way she did her job.

Besides that, sometime in my final year, I had struggled with a particular mandatory course so badly that I contemplated dropping it that semester. Troubled, I stopped by the office of a faculty adviser, Dr. Ezeife to seek her advice. After counselling me with many words, she left me with these final words which still resound in my head till this day; it sounded something like - "... if other students can excel in this course, you also can. You've got what it takes..." I remember leaving her office that day with an overwhelming peace and courage to take up the gauntlet. That semester ended up pretty well for me (that was actually my last semester).

The support and advice of academic advisers will play a reasonable part in your academic success. Don't forget to take note of the availability of the academic advisers and drop by their office whenever needed.

4. Career adviser:

While in post-secondary school, you shouldn't think about the academic realm only but the career realm as well. This is especially necessary if you plan on securing either a regular job after graduation or a co-op job during your studies. To this end, it is strongly recommended that you have regular discussions with your career advisers.

Career advisers can assist you with topics ranging from critiquing your résumé and cover letter and preparing you for job interviews, to guiding you on job search and suggesting relevant skills to acquire. They have your best interest at heart and will rejoice with you when you get that dream job. Your success is their success as well, so as much as possible leverage their assistance.

Talking about career advisers, I'll feel very guilty ending this section without mentioning one of my career advisers back in my undergrad days. Sometime in my second year at university, I faced a hard time securing a job while participating in the Co-operative Education (co-op) program; three months went by, and still I didn't get hired. Disappointing as it was, I remained in the program despite the fact that a couple of my friends had opted out from it and had attempted to persuade me to do the same. Later on, in that academic year, I was introduced to Mr. J. Quinlan, by an academic adviser and that was how our frequent, transformative meetings kicked off. He challenged me to release and to maximize my potentials and taught me a lot about the Canadian workplace culture which as an immigrant I had been oblivious to. In his own words, he had to continuously "pour hot coffee on me" because then, I was frozen in the ice of shyness and timidity - traits that weren't supportive of my career success (the ice is liquid now by the way). His efforts paid off as in the next semester; I secured a lucrative job which opened doors to other great opportunities.

Career advisers will labour to bring out the star in you as you work together with them. As usual, be sure to record their availability hours and pay them a visit whenever the need arises.

5. International Student Centre Staff:

Most schools have an International Student Centre which is usually referred to as a home away from home for the international students, and truly it is. The staff at the centre organizes events throughout each semester to bring the international students together to have fun and to shield them from frequent attacks of homesickness. These events may include movie night, pizza night, Christmas party, dog therapy day (on the week before final exams, therapy dogs are brought into a room where exams-nervous students enters to be calmed down by the dogs and wished good luck), host family program (for this one, families invite international students over to their homes on special occasions for example Christmas). These are just a few of the many fun events put together by the staff at the centre, and apparently these events are open to students who are interested.

These are some key resources which will undoubtedly benefit you. Remember also to make good use of the gym, bookstore, library, laboratories and the other facilities constructed to help you achieve success on this journey. Besides, you already paid for these services, so use them well.

How to make the most of lectures

First off, I enjoin you to attend lectures and not miss any - not even one - if you can help it. For one thing, you paid for it so why deprive yourself of your entitlement? Furthermore, it can be difficult to feel confident about yourself on a particular course when you've not been consistent with the lectures. (Imagine being very infrequent in class that by halfway down the semester the prof thinks you've just recently joined the class.)

Having said that, here are some things you can do to gain the most from lectures:

1. Preview lecture materials beforehand:

Especially when new material is to be covered, it will do you much good to visit the lecture slides and/or go over the assigned reading before going into the lecture. Doing this will at least get you familiar with the main points that'll be covered and possibly make you mindful of new, strange terminologies. This way you are more likely to follow through on the lecture and not get lost right from the beginning.

2. Find a distraction-free, comfy spot:

Most lecture rooms at state universities and colleges are usually large, sitting about hundreds of students (not necessarily to the extent of overcrowding though). Since there will be a bunch of students in there doing their own thing (for example chatting, texting, facebooking, tweeting, gaming, and possibly snoring), be sure to find a sitting position where you can hear and focus on the professor. Usually, the first few rows are the best places to sit, but I think most students aren't comfortable securing those spots. One more thing though: in as much as you want to avoid disturbing and distracting neighbours, you also shouldn't be a source of distraction and disturbance either.

3. Pay close attention to the prof:

Being able to hear the prof from your seat in the lecture hall is great - but not good enough. You may be hearing the voice of the prof, but then your mind is strolling in the mall, cafeteria or party venue. Hearing on its own happens on an unconscious level, but listening is a conscious activity. So then, listen attentively to the prof and guard against the strolling mind. Besides that, listen more carefully to the start and the end of the lecture. Most profs begin each lecture with a recap of the main points of the previous lecture and end with a summary of the main points that just got covered in the lecture. You don't want to miss out on any of those moments.

4. Take good notes:

Once you've got your focus locked onto the prof, keep your ears wide open for main points as you take down notes. Together with the main points, be sure to take note of definitions, examples, opinions, questions or problems (they may show up on tests or exams - you never know), differences, similarities, theorems, and applications of key concepts on the lecture - as well as useful exams hints that the prof may give away during the lecture.

Most times you can tell how vital certain points are by noticing how much emphasis the prof places on them. The prof could repeat certain words or concepts over, again and again, discuss particular points at length, or raise the tone of his or her voice while stating certain buzzwords which can be hinted by words like, "Take note of this ...", or "The meat of the point is ..." That's just the prof's way of saying, "Ok guys, it is essential that you take note of this point and digest it really well." The statements they make in any of those cases shouldn't be missing in your notes.

Remember you are only taking notes of key points and not jotting verbatim every word the prof utters. Since you'll be revisiting your notes, make sure you understand every word you write down. One more thing: for your notes, don't depend at all on only the outline on the lecture slides; focus on what the prof says instead.

By the way, did you know that taking notes during lecture is a kinesthetic action which is known to assist with memory? Therefore, coming to lecture with no writing materials or a laptop isn't a great idea.

5. Ask questions:

Don't hesitate to ask questions based on the prof's talk. As soon as any doubt or confusion pops up in your mind – just let it out immediately. If you hold back on doubts or complex ideas, your mind will unconsciously wander about trying to make meaning of them and - guess what? While this is happening, your level of concentration on the prof will likely drop. If you are shy to ask questions during lectures, you can let out any unclear idea by penning it down and then seeing the prof after the class. In any case, I think you should ask the question during the lecture once the doubt or unclear thought surfaces your mind, as it might help other students too. You may not be the only one who did not understand.

6. Engage in class discussions:

There is a Chinese proverb that says, "Tell me, and I'll forget. Show me, and I may remember. Involve me, I'll understand." With this in mind, you should consider getting involved in class discussions as they are a sure way to understand lecture materials. In addition, you'll be gradually wearing off any traits of timidity or shyness as you do this.

7. Revise lecture notes:

Right after the lecture, take the time to go over the lecture notes you've just compiled. If you had missed a line or two from the prof, then be sure to find out what those are and fill in your notes to keep them complete (a colleague in the class or the prof can help with this). Again, unless you have back-to-back lectures, endeavour to visit your lecture notes right after the lecture or once you are done with lectures for the day. One of the main reasons you want to do this is to quickly gauge your level of understanding of the lecture materials as you assimilate useful points discussed during the lecture. You gauge your level of understanding so that you can determine what you need to seek help on and what you need to practice some more times in order to grasp fully. The truth of the matter is that the more you visit the lecture materials, the more familiar you get with them and the higher your retention rate and understanding of the content; consequently, the higher your chances of acing your courses.

Furthermore, right after a lecture is a good time to start impressing those new concepts onto the walls of your mind so that by exam time you already have a solid grasp of those concepts. Apart from that, you want to do this to clear up all unclear concepts from the lecture before attending the next lecture where you may encounter even new, unfamiliar concepts. Accumulating concepts which you have not fully understood, from various lectures and waiting to clarify them just one or two days before an exam is strongly discouraged as you'll likely not be best prepared for the exam. Handle every doubt or uncertainty as they come - don't delay.

Start with the winning habits

Maintaining all-round success at school never happens by chance. It is usually the result of consistently carrying out series of actions which later become habits. From my observations so far, I've discovered that highly effective students possess winning habits that are supportive of their academic career success. Do you care to know what those habits are? If so, then read on.

Highly effective and successful students:

1. Schedule their time properly:

Having recognized that time is precious, highly effective students plan their time properly to ensure that they complete all required tasks before the deadlines. They strategically map out time to study for tests and exams in advance, complete assignments and projects early, revise lecture notes after lectures and still make out time for some fun. Keeping such schedules not only helps to identify the tasks to be done, but it also helps in organizing those tasks in order of priority; this way the most urgent and important tasks get done before the others. (See how to create effective schedules in Chapter 4 under "Map out the strategic plans.) When you work with schedules, you are more organized and able to do the right things at the right time.

2. Are up for the challenge:

Top students practice the saying that if you only do what you can do, you'll never be better than what you are (I got that line from Master Shifu in Kung Fu Pandu 3). These folks don't just remain in their comfort zone by taking easy courses; instead, they take courses that'll stretch their intellect and resistance level because they know that's the only way to grow.

3. Set goals:

Top students are goal setters; they know where they currently are and where they want to be in the future. They recognize their purpose (think in terms of the school life plan discussed in Chapter 1) and critical improvement areas in the various aspects of their lives (academic, financial, social, spiritual and so forth) and then create SMART goals to achieve their desires in those areas (SMART goals are covered in Chapter 4).

4. Have a positive mental attitude:

Highly successful students maintain a positive mental attitude. They understand that in order to succeed in the physical world, they must first succeed in the mental world. Though they encounter several hits of failure along the way, they realize that failure is neither fatal nor final. Brian Tracy, a success expert, once admonished, "Above all, you must maintain a positive mental attitude, looking for the good in every situation, and remain determined to be a completely positive person." A positive mental attitude is the exact type of attitude you require to excel at school. (See "Maintain a positive mental attitude" in Chapter 5 for tips on this area.)

5. Associate with other top students:

Have you noticed that we tend to become or act more like the people we hang out with the most? That explains why highly successful students flock together with other top students (and possibly with other smarter students). By modelling their success habits, and exchanging ideas and strategies amongst themselves, these flocks of high-achieving folks enjoy the benefits of synergy. Besides that, by the Law of Attraction which states, "like attract like," it's also clear why top students are more apt to gravitate towards those of their own caliber. I am convinced beyond any iota of doubt that if you make it a habit of associating more with students who are both at the same and at a higher level of success than you are, you'll definitely become more successful.

6. Practice self-discipline:

Highly successful students do what they say they'd do whether they feel like doing it or not. They study when they say they would (and not go to the mall with friends instead), they attend their morning lectures even when the temptation arises to sleep in, and they refuse to yield to suggestions that conflict with their values and belief. Top students keep up with their habit of self-discipline till the very end, till victory is won - whatever victory is, either short term or long term (that is persistence - self-discipline in action).

The amazing thing about self-discipline is that when applied in one area of your [school] life, success in that one area will trigger a series of successes in other areas. That's how come you can achieve all-round success when you begin applying self-discipline. By mastering self-discipline, you'll be opening the door to achieving a high level of self-esteem and self-confidence.

7. Commit to excellence:

A rather famous wise man, Deepak Chopra, once said, "If you focus on success you'll have stress. But if you pursue excellence, success will follow you." Hence, in whatever you do, be it – completing an assignment or project, writing a paper, preparing for an exam, delivering a presentation, working at a part-time or co-op job, spearheading a club event, and the list goes on - make sure to put in the best of your ability and capability because that's exactly what top students do. Choose to make excellence your brand, and you'll distinguish yourself amongst your peers.

8. Maximize the use of available resources:

On campus, knowing what resources are available to help you excel at school is highly essential. Not only do top students identify these resources, but they also put them to best use. (For more on this, see "How to make the most of the available resources on campus" – here in this chapter.) You paid for these resources so you may as well just maximize them and not let your tuition fees waste away.

9. Learn from failures and mistakes:

No one is perfect and, of course, that also includes the best of the top students. But one thing highly successful students do differently is to take account of their failures and mistakes to gain insight from them. Here is a good example of what I mean: whenever highly effective students get their exam or test or assignment papers back, so long as they didn't score a 100%, they make sure to find out what they did wrong to have lost some marks. They meet with the prof or TA or GA to help clarify comments on their exam if necessary, learn what exactly they didn't do right and ask how to best answer the question they had missed. This applies to assignments and projects as well. Finding your mistakes and reason for failure or mediocre pass marks is the first step to making improvements.

10. Take good care of themselves:

Balance, balance, balance. Top students balance their school life so that while they attend to their academic work, other areas of their school life (health, spiritual, financial, emotional, and social) aren't jeopardized. (See more on balancing your school life in Chapter 6.) The truth is that ignoring one or more of the non-academic areas of the school life can negatively impact your academic work. For example, not maintaining proper sanitation and eating unhealthy can lead to illness which can affect one's academic performance.

Cultivate these habits and watch your performance at school skyrocket. The good thing here is that these success habits, once developed, can be transferred to later stages of your life after you graduate from school, so you won't be wasting your effort and time working to develop them now. Goal setting is one of the success habits practised by highly effective students. Top students don't just set goals; they set SMART goals which obviously are way better than mere goals. To learn more about SMART goals move on to the next chapter. (Don't forget the "Roll up your sleeves" exercises though.)

Roll up your sleeves

1. Find out the date for your orientations and commit to attending them.
2. Take note of the office hours of your professors and TAs & GAs for the courses you are enrolled for this semester.
3. Check out the availability of your career and academic advisers and be sure to drop by their office when the need arises.
4. If you are an international student, visit the International Student Centre at your school (the staff there will be glad to meet you).
5. Resolve to maximally utilize the facilities (gym, library, laboratories, etc.) on campus.
6. Looking at the 10 habits of highly effective students presented in this chapter, be sure to maintain and reinforce those you've

cultivated already. Find out which ones you lack or are weak at
and take action today to strengthen your weak area(s).

CHAPTER FOUR

Set SMART goals

*"Set daily, monthly, and long-term goals and
dreams. Don't ever be afraid to dream too big.
Nothing is impossible. If you believe in
yourself, you can achieve it. "*
~~ Nastia Liukin

I once heard the story of a man who watched a friend play the darts game (the one where a player throws darts into a bullseye on a dartboard positioned on a wall some distance away). As this man watched closely, he noticed that his friend kept missing the bullseye on every throw of the darts. So this man moved near his friend and gently asked him the reason for the disappointing misses. To his surprise, the response he got was, "the bullseye isn't my target. I was never aiming at it which was why I never hit it." Returning to his original position, the man continued watching the player but this time with happiness over the successful misses. The moral of the scene isn't so complicated, and it is this: whatever you don't aim at, you'll likely miss. In other words, to guarantee that you'll hit something, you have to aim at it. This probably sounds like something you are familiar with - G-O-A-L! One of the required skills that will help you achieve success on your academic journey is goal setting. In fact, its benefits can't be overemphasized, and you'll need this skill not only at school but more so at your job or wherever you choose to go after your graduation.

In this chapter, you'll learn how to set SMART goals that will enable you to achieve just about any objective you desire. In addition, you'll learn how to map out strategic plans to facilitate the accomplishment of your set goals. By the way, are you wondering what SMART stands for? Just read on!

Before I proceed to discuss SMART goals, I want to demonstrate to you why it is essential to set goals for yourself and how it can affect your success.

A case study on goal setting

In 1979, a case study was carried out among graduates from Harvard Business School, and the result was fascinating. Of the people who were interviewed, 84% had no definite goals (let's call them group A), 13% had definite goals but didn't pen down their goals (group B), and only 3% committed their goals to writing (group C). Ten years later, it was discovered that those in group B, the 13% folks, were earning, on average, 2 times more than those in group A, the 84% folks. Much more intriguing was the fact that the folks in group C, the 3% group, were earning, on average, 10 times more than the remaining 97%. [1] Wow! Now that is fascinating!

Hopefully, those figures have convinced you of the importance of setting goals and writing them down. I perceive already that you are ready to begin penning down your goals; but before you do that, let me give you some solid tips to make your goals really effective.

Make them SMART

You may have noticed how a couple of gadgets in our world are becoming smart and hence more reliable. For example, smartphones, smart fridge, smart toys, and other smart gizmos that are making life more convenient for humans. What then would you think of SMART goals? First of all, goals, as you know, drive us toward achieving our desires; therefore by making them SMART, we can be more confident and sure of reaching our dreams.

Here is what I mean when I say SMART [goals]:
Specific
Measurable
Achievable
Realistic
Time-bound

Specific

Your goals must be specific. They must state precisely what you plan to achieve and how you intend to achieve it. For example, merely saying, "I want to do well on my upcoming Math test," isn't good enough. Rather you should say something like:

"I obtain an A+ (91% and above) on my Calculus 101 course this semester. To achieve this, I score at least 92 % on my midterm exams, quizzes, and the final exam."

Being specific about your goals helps you define your bullseye which you can see clearly enough to hit. Notice the use of the present tenses - "I obtain..." and "I score..." – as though the goal were achieved already. Using such words especially in goal setting awakens the subconscious mind, and makes it work on ways to achieve the set goal. The more you feed your subconscious mind with your specific goals, the harder it works to produce definite possibilities for achieving your goals.

One more thing I must mention is that while you expect the best, you should plan for the worst. Les Brown implied this when he remarked, "Shoot for the moon, and if you miss, you will still be among the stars." I'll connect the dots with an illustration. Suppose you have an intention to score an A+ (say, 91% and above) on an upcoming test, preferably you want to aim higher than 91%, so say, 95%. This way, in the event, that an unprecedented occurrence happens and you don't make 95%; you'll likely not miss 91%. (That is a good strategy I tell you!)

Measurable

The only way you can tell whether or not a goal has been achieved is if you can precisely track your progress toward reaching it. This aspect is crucial because it clearly shows you how far or near you are from approaching your goal. Also, it tells you how much effort you need to apply towards the accomplishment of the task at hand. For example, setting a goal of acing your Calculus 101 course - by scoring at least 92% on all assessments (i.e. midterm, quizzes, and final exam) - gives you an idea of how much you should study (and stay on your knees) in preparing for the test. By attaching a specific percentage to each assessment, it becomes simple to know whether or not you are on track. Just as you can easily keep track of the money in your piggy-bank or wallet, you should be able to easily measure your goals and keep track to stay on course.

Achievable

A goal, though may be high, should be achievable; it may be beyond your reach but mustn't be beyond your sight. This means that your goal should be challenging enough that it makes you stretch and keeps you out of your comfort zone (that is the only way you can grow). Going back to the sample goal stated earlier - "I obtain an A+ (91% and above) on my Calculus 101 course ..." Scoring an A+ on an upcoming Math test, at first, may look daunting, but come to think about it, how do you know that this goal, for instance, is achievable? The philosopher Bertrand Russell provided an answer to the question when he once wrote, "The very best proof that something can be done is that someone else has already done it." A lot of students before you have scored an A+ on the seemingly toughest courses at school. That is why I know that you can ace any course if you make it your goal. This applies to any goal you have in mind, be it in the area of health and fitness, spiritual, mental, intellectual, and what have you. You know you can do it because others have done it before (even if others haven't you still can become the trailblazer).

While you ponder on that, also remember that whatever the mind can conceive and believe it can achieve (that's originally from Napoleon Hill). If you can think it, you can achieve it!

Realistic

There is a limit to what can be done at any time period given known conditions. So, when setting your goals, understand what limits exist and set your goals within the known restrictions. For example, you can't set a goal to obtain a final grade of 80% on an English course when you had scored below 65% on your three previous assessments. (I am assuming here that the final grade is the average of the three assessments.) Honestly, such a goal won't be realistic (considering no makeup tests and no miracles), and you may end up getting disappointed with yourself if you don't adjust the goal to make it feasible.

Sometime during my undergrad, I had set a goal at the beginning of the semester, as was my practice, to obtain a final grade of A+ on one of the courses I had enrolled in. Unfortunately, I didn't do as well as I had expected on my two midterm exams. Having done the math and seen how unrealistic obtaining an "A+" was, before facing the final exam, I decided to pull down my target from an "A+" to an "A" instead. In the end, I wasn't disappointed. That's what I meant when I referred to considering existing limits or restrictions at a given time period.

From the story I just shared, the restriction that existed at that period of the semester was that my first two assessments weren't good enough to birth the initial goal I had set – an "A+." So, I had to work with what I had (the midterm scores) which meant dropping my goal to an "A" which was finally realized. Following that experience, I re-resolved to starting strong and well, each semester, by hitting the highest score possible upfront.

Time-bound

When you set a goal, you want to have a time when you can say for sure that your goal has been achieved. Simply put, you need to assign a deadline to your goal as affirmed by Napoleon Hill when he said, "a goal is a dream with a deadline."

Let us refer back to the example of scoring a 91% on a Calculus 101 course. It is clear that by about two or three weeks after the day of the final exam you should know whether or not your goal has been attained. (Hopefully, the course professor doesn't keep you in suspense.) In a situation where you set a goal to complete an assignment by a given date, say 3 days before it is due, you know certainly whether or not the goal has been attained when that day comes. There is a saying that there is no such thing as an unattainable goal, there is only an unattainable deadline. The fact that you didn't complete an assignment by a set deadline, for example, only implies that the deadline wasn't realistic or on point. It doesn't mean that you can't complete the assignment.

You may not always meet all the deadlines you set, but that shouldn't deter you from setting another and another after that. Also, never say you'll complete an assignment or a task "someday" or at "some time" because "someday" means "no day" and "some time" translates to "no time." Having deadlines for your goals or tasks arms you against the villain of procrastination which you should conquer lest it conquers you. The more you practice the habit of setting a deadline, the more accurate you become at setting and meeting your deadlines and ultimately achieving your goals

Kick off each semester with SMART goals

I have seen several war movies where an army of warriors are arrayed for battle and are ready to storm the battlefield. One thing I have noticed is that even before the army is set, a strategy must have been long devised and mastered by all the warriors, and only then can victory be hoped for and guaranteed. The bottom line is that the best time to strategize is before the battle and not while the battle is already heated up.

You may already know where I am going. Yes, the same applies to your academic journey (or academic battle, if you wish). The best time to begin setting your goals and strategizing is right at the onset of the semester when you're at your best and aren't staggering under the weight of school work. Waiting until the middle of the semester to set your goals isn't ideal because you may already feel demotivated by unexpected events around you. Apparently, the end of the semester can't be a good time to set your goals either unless the goals are meant for the next semester. When you set your goals and strategize plans, which will be discussed later in this chapter, you give yourself the motivation needed to keep going through the semester and beyond.

Precisely, at the beginning of each semester, after you must have known the timetable for your courses, you should move on to define your goal(s) for each course. For example, say, one of the courses you are taking is **Introduction to Biology;** you should compose your goal statement for the course as described earlier in the chapter. After you must have listed the courses, you are taking in the semester, write beside each course, your expected letter grade or score. Maintaining a daily planner or a diary (or a smartphone app or whatever works for you) will prove useful here.

Here is an example from a top student named Hermoine (yes, maybe the one from Harry Potter movie):

Course (Course code)	Expected grade by the end of the semester
Introduction to Biology (BIO101)	A-
Differential Calculus (CALC200)	B+
Introduction to Business (BIZ101)	A+
Social Psychology (PSYC201)	A

Hermoine's course goals

53

Remember to keep it clear and straightforward. It also helps to visit these goals frequently if possible once daily, or as often as will keep you from forgetting them. (In subsequent sections of this chapter, reference will be made to the courses in the table above.) This is an excellent way to keep you focused on your goals throughout the semester. You'd want to compose your goal statements and categorize them into long-term and short-term goals which will be discussed next. This exercise will equip you on your school journey (or battle as I like to refer to it), reminding you that no one else but you alone should win the battle.

Long-term and short-term [SMART] goals

For about three and half years during my undergrad studies, I had the privilege of officially mentoring students, through my participation in a mentorship program on campus. On my first encounter with my mentees, I would help them think through and structure their goals, making their goals as SMART as possible. We would also work together to group the goals into two categories namely: short-term goals and long-term goals. After that, we would devise strategies to achieve the set goals. And yes, the names of these types of goals depend on their nature. Short-term goals typically have a deadline spanning days, weeks or even months whereas long-term goals can be a matter of semesters or an academic year or a program year, as your strategy dictates.

Here are some examples of short-term and long-term goals:

S/N	Long-term goals	Short-term goals
1	"I graduate with a distinction (i.e. with a cumulative grade point average, GPA, between 80-90%, for example). To achieve this, I maintain an average of nothing less than 85% each academic year."	"I maintain a grade average of 86% on all my courses by the end of the semester. I plan to score at least 88% on my two midterm tests and then 87% on my final exam." (I assumed here that the overall score is an average of the three assessments.)
2	"By the first semester of my 3rd year, I am the vice president of the student services on campus. To attain this, I gain experience and exposure within the student service system on campus by joining the student board this semester being the second semester in my second year."	"By next semester, I am a board member of the student services on campus. I increase my visibility on campus by participating in events organized by student groups around campus. To this end, I seek the advice of board members and executives as well even as I prepare to submit my application for the position before the end of the week."

From the sample goals above, you can see how the long-term goals are broken down to form the short-term goals which could be broken down further if need be. Breaking down your goals makes them easy to manage and track. Generally speaking, you should have at least one goal for the various aspects of your life as in - academic, social, spiritual, physical and health - so you can achieve the all-round success you desire.

The goal setting technique that changes life

During my undergrad, I participated in a mentorship program called "Connecting4Success" where lower-year students get paired up with a higher-year student who would serve as a mentor. Through the program, I had the privilege of mentoring students and helping them create goals and devise plans to accomplish those goals. I have asked one of my mentees, Joel Wellington, to share his experience adopting the SMART goal-setting technique which was a fundamental part of the program. Here is what Joel has to say:

We all start out from childhood with a dream and a purpose of becoming something in future and that happens to be our goal and our drive to succeed. When I got into the university, I had one, a fire and a drive to succeed, something I have always had my entire life, but I really didn't understand a lot till I joined the "Connecting4success" program.

Through the program and with the aid of my mentor, I learnt a lot about goals that I never knew. I got to learn about Specific, Measurable, Achievable, Realistic, Time-bound goals as well as long-term and short-term goals. Funny enough, I had only considered long-term goals, but never short-term goals which were equally important as well. Getting to know this, I was able to plan, create both long-term and short-term goals, and make sure to hit my targets. If for some reason I didn't strike the target, I would look at my mistakes and try to avoid them next time.

Sometime in the second semester of my undergrad, I had set goals to attain an 'A+' in my courses. Unfortunately, I came out with some 'B+'s and 'B's. I later was able to identify where I went wrong and it was due to unplanned events like late assignment and missing assignments. After tightening things up a bit more with the SMART goal-setting technique, I ended up achieving everything I had planned on paper for that semester.

In fact, till date, I apply the SMART goal-setting technique even outside school. Recently, I had to pay off a significant sum of money, and I never thought I could get this out of the way quick enough. Instead of worrying about how to get the money, I decided to set up a plan based on the SMART goals I had created. I broke down the big, long-term goal into smaller, short-term goals and noticed that if I could save a certain amount of money every day, I would achieve my overall goal. Honestly speaking, I didn't even realize when I hit the target, but I ended up achieving my set goal soon enough. From that incident, I got convinced of the power of setting goals and writing them down. Whenever you do that, it becomes a reminder to you every minute until you have achieved your goals.

The SMART goal-setting technique isn't meant for the school life alone, but actually for life in general. When you learn it and apply it correctly to an area of your life, you will be amazed at the impossible things you can achieve. Ever since I learnt about this technique from my mentor, it has been an integral part of my life. Every decision I make appears to be based on that technique, and I know that for the rest of my life I will continue to apply the SMART goal-setting technique.

Map out the strategic plans

A goal without a plan, they say, is just a wish. Thus, after setting goals, the next step is to create concrete plans, in the form of schedules, to actualize those goals. The schedules will contain the activities you intend to carry out each day, week, and a semester in order to meet your goals. By practising the act of organizing and planning [your schedule], you'll be cultivating good time management and prioritization skills which will be very useful even past the walls of your school.

Talking about organizing and planning your schedules, it always helps to start with the bigger picture then narrow down into the smaller pixels. For the sake of simplicity, I'll take the bigger picture to be a semester schedule (or plan) and the smaller pixels to be a daily schedule; the weekly schedule, which falls in between, will be discussed as well.

First of all, I recommend that you get a calendar or a planner; be it an app on a smartphone or a paper calendar; find one that is handy and suits you best. That said, here is what the semester schedule is about.

Semester schedule

When you have a good picture of what an entire semester holds, you'll feel a sense of control; the semester schedule is aimed at providing that picture. The semester schedule isn't anything complex; it's just a calendar or planner that will contain an entry for all the major or minor events that you'll be involved in for a given semester. Such events can range from midterm or final exams, project or assignment deadlines to birthday party of friends or family, reading week break, and so forth. Having all these events in one place makes it easy to see what's coming up and how you can start getting set for it. It also assists with deciding how to assign priorities to the various events.

Here is a scenario where the semester schedule can be useful. Let's suppose that you have a paper due on a particular day, say, on a Wednesday by 11:59 PM and a friend had invited you to a birthday party on Tuesday, i.e. the day before the paper's deadline. If both events were considered major and vital to you, they should be noted on your semester schedule (i.e. your calendar) early enough so you can attend to both. Preferably, you may want to complete the paper by Monday or before the party to make room for unforeseen circumstances, so you don't miss the deadline for the paper on Wednesday. However, if for some reasons you didn't start your paper until Monday night because you hadn't pinned its deadline on your semester schedule, then you'll have to decide based on your priority whether to: ignore the deadline of the paper and go for your friend's party or explain your situation to your friend and complete your paper before the deadline. If you are fortunate enough, you could get the paper done and still make it to the party. But doing things at the last moment is not a habit you want to live by - trust me! The bottom line is that maintaining a semester schedule will help you see ahead and plan ahead.

In as much as it is great to list every possible event on your calendar, you'll agree with me that some occurrences are unprecedented and out of your control. For example, an impromptu birthday party for a friend or family member, a surprise outing with friends, etc. can derail your plans. You can plan for such occurrences by leaving some empty slots on your calendar. Having margins on your calendar helps keep you flexible to a large extent.

With all these said, here is a sample semester schedule used by a top student, Hermoine:

WINTER SEMESTER SCHEDULE 2015

JANUARY 2015

SUN	MON	TUE	WED	THU	FRI	SAT
				1	2	3
4	5 Classes begin	6	7	8 Mom's bday	9	10
11	12	13	14	15	16	17
18	19 PSYC asn 1 due	20	21	22	23	24
25	26 BIO asn1 due	27 PSYC asn 2 due	28	29	30	31 CALC asn 1 due

FEBRUARY 2015

SUN	MON	TUE	WED	THU	FRI	SAT
1	2	3 PSYC asn 3 due	4 Mark's bday	5 BIZ asn1 due	6	7 BIZ midterm 1
8	9 BIO midterm 1	10	11 CALC midterm 1	12 PSYC midterm 1	13	14 CALC asn 2 due
15	16	17	18	19	20	21
22	23 PSYC asn 4 due	24 READING WEEK	25	26	27	28 CALC asn 3 due

MARCH 2015

SUN	MON	TUE	WED	THU	FRI	SAT
1	2	3	4	5	6	7
8	9 BIO midterm 2	10	11	12	13	14 BIZ midterm 2 CALC asn 4 due
15	16 PSYC asn 7 due	17 CALC midterm 2	18	19	20	21
22	23 PSYC asn 8 due	24	25 BIO asn 2 due	26	27	28 my bday CALC asn 5 due
29	30	31				

APRIL 2015

SUN	MON	TUE	WED	THU	FRI	SAT
				1	2	3	4 Philip's bday
5	6 Last day of Classes	7	8	9	10	11
12 PSYC final	13	14	15 BIO final	16	17	18
19	20 BIZ final	21 CALC Final	22	23	24	25
26	27	28	29	30		

Hermoine's Semester Schedule

61

Notice how the following entries were included: deadlines for assignments and projects, midterms and final exams dates. You should have access to those dates by the first 2-3 weeks into the semester or even earlier. The dates for the midterm and final exams should be available to you right from day one of the semesters on the school's student portal (this system should be your best companion so try to familiarize yourself with it as soon as you can). However, for the deadlines of the assignments and projects, the professors will direct you to where to find those (probably on the course website).

Looking at the sample semester schedule above, I want to draw your attention to some series of interesting events:

1. Back-to-back midterms and exams:

You see how between February 10th and 12th, midterms for BIO, CALC and PSYC were closely lined up? If proper planning isn't done, that period would be a very stressful one. So, watch out for such back-to-back midterms and exams, and strategize your reading plan such that you are prepared for the individual exams.

I believe that a student is expected to begin preparing for an exam at least a week prior; (I know of several professors and top students who actually agree with me on that too). What I mean here is that you can't wait until one or two days before a Calculus midterm, for example, to begin learning to differentiate or integrate higher-order functions. You should cultivate the habit of learning new materials way earlier and then practising regularly to get better and more comfortable with those. You may be super-smart that you can learn the course materials just the day before the exam, but then if an unforeseen event that leaves you unfit to study hits you, you'll likely be in a dire situation.

So again, 1-2 days would hardly ever be enough to fully prepare for an exam especially if one hasn't been keeping up with course materials from day one.

In the section on a weekly schedule, I'll share some insights on how to proactively keep up with course materials.

2. Early and plenty of assignments:

From Hermoine's semester schedule above, you may be surprised to see that assignment 1 for PSYC is due just 2 weeks after the first day of classes. This means that the assignment was handed out on either the same or the following week after the classes began (welcome to college and university). Believe me; this is real. I remember receiving assignments in my first lecture for a couple of courses during my undergrad days. Just keep an eye on courses like this. (Please note that I only used PSYC as an example. It doesn't mean that you'll have such early and plenty of assignments if you choose to take a PSYC course.) As I had suggested earlier in this chapter, get prepared for the semester as early as you can so you are not caught unawares by such surprising, early deadlines.

Please note that the sample semester schedule provided here is only meant to serve as a guide. Feel free to add as many other major or minor events as it can hold. Having a clear picture of important events in an entire semester at one glance will undoubtedly help you plan each semester more accurately and give you a good sense of control of your time.

Now that the semester schedule is covered let's move onto the weekly schedule.

Weekly schedule

Each semester, you'll likely be involved in a routine each week. For instance, on Tuesday and Thursday, you may have lectures for 2 or 3 courses; then on Monday and Wednesday for another 2 or 3 courses and then for another course or 2 on Friday depending on your workload for the semester. It helps then to have a weekly timetable especially at the beginning of the semester when you are still trying to wrap your head around a lot of happenings around you.

Apart from including lectures into the weekly schedule, you also want to consider inserting activities such as working out in the morning, reviewing lecture after each class, praying and meditating, reading news related to your field, amongst many others. I found it extremely helpful to review lecture materials at the end of each lecture, if possible, immediately after each class. This is a proven way to get carried along on each course you are taking and to prepare for exams proactively.

Here is a weekly sample schedule:

WEEKLY SCHEDULE/TIMETABLE

	Monday	Tuesday	Wednesday	Thursday	Friday	Saturday	Sunday
08:00 AM					Workout		
08:30 AM	Workout		Workout				
09:00 AM						Study BIO	
09:30 AM		Workout		Workout			
10:00 AM					BIO LAB		
10:30 AM	PSYC lecture		PSYC lecture				
11:00 AM							Church
11:30 AM		BIO lecture		BIO lecture	CALC LAB		
12:00 AM							
12:30 PM	Review PSYC lecture		Review PSYC lecture				
01:00 PM							
01:30 PM		Review BIO lecture		Review BIO lecture		Study BIZ	
02:00 PM					Review BIO LAB		
02:30 PM							Study PSYC
03:00 PM							
03:30 PM	CALC lecture		CALC lecture		Review CALC LAB		
04:00 PM							
04:30 PM		BIZ lecture		BIZ lecture			
05:00 PM	Review CALC lecture		Review CALC lecture				
05:30 PM							
06:00 PM							Study CALC
06:30 PM		Review BIZ lecture		Review BIZ lecture			
07:00 PM					Meditation		
07:30 PM	Meditation		Meditation				
08:00 PM							
08:30 PM							
09:00 PM		Meditation		Meditation			
09:30 PM							
10:00 PM							
10:30 PM							

Hermoine's Weekly Schedule

Again the weekly schedule shown here is only meant to serve as a guide; you can add other entries to it. You can begin each day with quiet time for prayer and reflection followed by a workout session; that can be followed by, say, reading news update which can be carried out while having breakfast (apparently that's only after having your shower); these, of course, are not mandatory. Reading up news on your field will be useful if or when you plan to secure a co-op or regular job. You'll need to stay abreast of the current state of the market in your field to learn what skills are in high demand so you can begin equipping yourself.

The importance of reviewing your lecture materials after each class has been discussed earlier and that is why it isn't missing in the weekly schedule. Meditation can be in the form of reading an inspirational book such as the Bible or any self-help books, reflecting on your day or indulging in other mind-resting exercises. It is meant to relieve you of the day's pressure and give you time to evaluate your day.

One more thing to draw your attention to is the blank, empty slots that appear on the schedule. Those represent margins which you can dedicate to working on assignments, having your meals or other worthwhile activities. If you look carefully, you'll observe that no slots exist for bedtime or wake-up time; this was done on purpose. It is tough to say when students should go to bed or when they are to get off the bed. To tell the truth, some students hardly go to bed as they are almost always awake. What I can say here is that you should try as much as you can to have enough sleep. It is recommended that students get about 6-8 hours of sleep (a lot of students have a problem with that as they think it is too much). Irrespective of how much time you sleep, endeavour to stay active and alert during lectures, at the very least. You wouldn't want to be found nodding while the professor is speaking right in front of you. If this happens to you, then you really need to increase your sleeping hours to get sufficient rest.

Lectures typically don't hold during the weekend, but that doesn't mean that Saturdays and Sundays should be left unoccupied in the weekly schedule. Your weekend can be used to catch up on sleep, go to church, complete personal or assigned readings for your courses, work on assignments or projects, visit the mall, hang out with family and friends, cook (I always looked forward to weekends for this one) and for many other activities that will help you attain your overall goals. As seen in the schedule, you could dedicate Saturday to focus on two of your courses then the rest, on Sunday. Whatever you do, try not to leave your entire weekend completely open as this may not be the best use of your time.

Daily Schedule

Planning your day is just as important as planning your semester and your week since each day makes up the week which makes up the semester. It may not be ideal to simply wake up in the morning and walk out of your house without considering what activities you'll be doing and in what order they will be done. Keeping in mind your weekly and semester schedules, you may want to consider organizing a to-do list of tasks for your day. The best time to do this is either the night before or in the morning before starting out the day when you still have the whole day ahead of you.

Here is an example, as usual:

No.	Tasks for Tuesday 3 rd Feb. 2015
1	Submit PSYC asn 3
2	Work on BIZ asn 1 (due on Thursday)
3	Meet with a prof for BIZ to clarify unclear concepts from study time on Saturday
4	Start preparing for BIZ midterm (this Saturday); review Chapters 1&2 of the textbook
5	Buy birthday card for Mark (His bday is tomorrow)

Hermoine's daily schedule for Tuesday 3rd Feb. 2015

You'll notice that the entries in the above list agree with the weekly and semester schedule. For example, according to the semester schedule, PSYC assignment (asn) 3 is due on Tuesday, 3rd February 2015. As you can see from the to-do list above, the first task for the day is to submit that assignment. You can submit it days before which will be great, but this is only an example. Also, the plan was made to begin preparing for BIZ midterm 1 coming up on Saturday, 7th February 2015. In order to avoid duplicating entries already in the weekly schedule such as meditation and lectures, those aren't included in the daily schedule for simplicity. These tasks on the daily schedule will fall into the blank time slots in the weekly schedule.

Try not to have too many tasks for a given day (for example, more than 10 if you can't handle it), so you don't get disappointed when you don't complete them all. At the same time don't yield to the temptation of having only a few tasks for a given day by pushing more tasks to a later day. It has been said several times, "Do not leave for tomorrow what you can do today." So then, do as much as you can do each day, knowing that the next day will come along with its own issues and tasks.

The scheduling strategy that works wonders

In the course of my undergrad, I had introduced the scheduling technique especially the weekly schedule discussed in this chapter to a friend of mine, Joanna Markiewicz. It produced incredible results in her life so I thought I should share her story (By the way, at the moment, Joanna is running her own business and living the entrepreneurial life she had always desired):

> The most significant success I've had in course work is when I applied the strategy of reviewing lecture notes right after lectures plus blocking off weekends to review lecture notes. Making the decision to do this drastically changed my ability to understand and remember the lectures. With that, I was able to exponentially increase my marks.
>
> It's amazing how a few simple habits throughout the day can make such a difference in overall results. The great Jim Rohn defines failure as a few errors in judgement repeated every day. If that is the case, then a few good choices each day will lead to success! You don't have to be really smart to do well in school; you just have to decide to do a few of the right simple tasks each day. Anyone can do it, and it is worth it. Someone once said that the greatest victory you can have in life is the one you have over yourself. Victory over myself produces great joy in my life and increases my productivity in all aspects of life.
>
> Decide today to implement one small positive daily task, stay consistent and see what happens.

Wrapping up on schedules

Organizing daily, weekly and semester schedules may look

burdensome and difficult at first, but I can assure you that they are good investments. As you continue steadfastly with this exercise, it will become fun especially as their fruits become evident. In general, schedules (i.e. daily, weekly and semester schedules) are meant to liberate you not limit you. They will help save you the risk of forgetting about important events. The pressure and mental bombardments each school day brings are enough to knock off entries from your mental schedule (i.e. schedule organized in your mind). Written (or physical) schedules, as shown in this chapter, are necessary and have no alternatives - not even mental schedule.

The act of organizing and planning your schedules to achieve your goals is a transferable skill which will surely benefit you whether you end up working for a company or running your own business. In addition, maintaining schedules will help you manage your time effectively. The daily schedule, for example, states what activities you are involved in each day. With that, you can wisely account for the use of every minute of every hour of every day. Besides that, you'll keep the momentum rolling as each day you'll be taking steps that will draw you closer to your goals.

With all these schedules in place, you'll be mindful of doing what you plan to do each day, each week and each semester. As you discipline yourself to set goals and achieve them, you'll respect and feel good about yourself. Eventually, you'll develop a high self-image, high self-esteem and great self-confidence, becoming the successful student you've always wanted to be.

Managing stress and pressure

"All work and no play," they say, "makes Jack dull." I am sure you are tired of hearing that saying, but nothing can be truer than it is. It helps to form the habit of following intense study times with intense play times (just don't overplay please). A student once commented on this topic by saying, "I work so hard at studying so that I can work so hard at playing."

After engaging in a marathon study in preparation for your midterm exam, you can choose to - hang out with friends, play video games (my favourite option), workout or watch a movie – to ease away your stress and feel refreshed again before moving on. The human mind desires such balance to function at its best. That is why you are encouraged to incorporate exercise into your daily routine at least for about 30-60 minutes, 5-7 times per week. Working out in the morning causes your body to release endorphins which make you feel good and active enough to start off your day well.

Besides that, you can minimize stress and tension by creating plans for completing the tasks at hand. I have come to realize that stress can arise when no possibilities for solving a problem are being explored. For example, suppose you have a midterm exam coming up in two days, and you are completely lost in the course materials which you'll be tested on. Not just that, assume that you didn't even think of how to get help and from whom to get help. Picture that moment for a bit, and you'll experience what tension blended with stress feels like. In the light of this, maintaining your daily, weekly and semester schedules will cut down the effect of stress by infusing confidence in you. I am hoping you'll make use of the discussed schedules.

You are now ready to activate the power of goal setting and planning into your school life. By putting these powerful tools into action, you'll achieve the goals you set for yourself.

In the next chapter, you'll be supplied with useful tips on how to obtain and maintain the GPA you've always desired.

Roll up your sleeves

1. What worthy goals, which when achieved, will give you maximum happiness at this moment?
    a. Write down 3-5 SMART (**S**pecific, **M**easurable, **A**chievable, **R**ealistic, **T**ime-bound) goals, specifying which are short-

term and long-term goals.

b. The goals can be in the area of health and fitness, academic, social, spiritual, mental, finance - basically, in any sphere you have identified as applicable and necessary.

2. Devise plans to achieve the goals you've just set by organizing your daily, weekly and semester schedules. You can use the sample schedules provided as a guide. (Try having these in place by the first few weeks of classes)

3. Resolve to manage stress by following intense work with play and by sticking to your schedules.

CHAPTER FIVE

Treasure the grades

"Success is no accident. It is hard work, perseverance, learning, studying, sacrifice and most of all love what you are doing.. "
~~ Pele

In universities and colleges, your GPA, i.e. Grade Point Average, is an indicator of your performance on the journey of your academic career. The GPA (more precisely cumulative GPA) is basically a cumulation of your grades for the courses you have completed. The grades get assigned from activities such as assignments, course exams (midterms and finals), papers, presentations, and projects (group or individual). Therefore, for you to keep your GPA afloat and to conquer the enemy of academic probation, you are required to do well on all of those activities.

In this chapter, I'll share with you handy tips on how to: study like an 'A' student, write effective papers, ace your exams, and handle demanding group projects appropriately.

Studying like an 'A' student

Successful students study effectively, and that's one of the main reasons they perform very well academically. Part of studying effectively involves having scheduled study times all through the week and not waiting until the night before an exam to cram. In fact, research shows that studying done bit by bit over a period of time is more effective than the one-time cramming on the night before an exam [1]. (Check out Hermoine's weekly schedule in Chapter 4 to see how you can incorporate study times into your weekly routine.)

That said, let's dive into key things you should consider when you want to study effectively:

1. Find the right environment:

You aren't restricted to studying only in the library or in your room or in some other specific place. The only thing that matters most is that the location you choose promotes concentration and is free from distraction. For example, bright lighting, minimal or no background sounds, room temperature, and so forth – all these make up an ideal environment for studying.

2. Shut off all distractions:

Having your cell phone, tablet or laptop with you while studying can be quite tempting. There is no way you won't pause your reading to check your phone when a new message comes in; not to talk of visiting Facebook, Twitter, Instagram, and other social media sites in the middle of your studying. Beware of these distractors. If you plan to study materials from a hard copy textbook, then I think it is a good idea not to take your laptop along with you to the study area. You can choose to do the same thing with your phone if you know your phone's got you. Otherwise, consider switching it off or turning it on silent mode, keeping it out of your sight and only looking for it once it's break-time or end of study time (don't worry you won't miss any urgent calls). If, however, you need your laptop to access an electronic copy of the reading material then try to restrict the number of tabs you have opened. Overcome the temptation of opening a tab for Facebook another for Instagram and yet another for who knows what. Self-discipline is key here. I know you can conquer these distractors.

3. **Stick to the required text**:

   For courses with more than one textbook, find out which one is the required text and which is only recommended. Unless you want to learn more about certain topics or concepts for a paper or simply for your understanding, you can pick up the recommended text; otherwise, you should be fine using the required text. Better still, you can confirm with the course professor on this.

4. **Skim through the objectives and summary first**:

   Before reading a chapter in a book, for example, it helps to first scan the objectives and the summary for new and unfamiliar concepts and words. This will give you an idea of what to expect in the text, the organization and structure of the chapter as well as the main points. Having knowledge of the main points from the start makes you aware of what's important so that you don't ignore them accidentally.

5. **Read with purpose**:

   When you pick up a book to read, always define your aim for reading. If you do so, it becomes possible and straightforward to tell whether or not that aim has been achieved by the end of the study time. Example of reading aims can range from reading to get the gist of text (more on the surface level), understanding specific concepts in preparation for an exam or a paper, amongst others. Whatever the case may be, have a purpose before jumping into the material.

6. Engage with the material:

To get the most when you read, think about the information you are gathering as you ask and attempt to answer the - What, When, How, Where, and Why – about concepts and ideas you come across. For example, say, you are reading a chapter on photosynthesis; inside your head, you should ask yourself questions such as: so what exactly is photosynthesis? When, how, where and why does it occur? (Those are only fundamental questions though; there are several complex questions on that topic.) Doing this will help you quickly grasp the relevant information.

7. Practice active reading:

Running your eyes through the words on the pages of a textbook while thinking about the content is a good place to start. However, supplementing that with kinesthetic actions such as – highlighting some key lines, scribbling on page margins, or writing into a note or onto flashcards - will boost your retention rate. When you take time to write and rewrite key definitions or explanations, or draw and redraw diagrams, you impress those more deeply into your memory; the end result is a sharp recall rate. (Obviously, it isn't a good idea to highlight or scribble on a borrowed textbook. Jotting into your notebook or flashcards will be better in such a case.)

8. Recognize and relate:

It is easier to remember information that is both meaningful and interesting to you. One way to quickly store new information into your memory is to relate it to existing and interesting ones. Since you aren't likely going to forget facts and information that are meaningful to you, by connecting those to new fact and information recall is eased. Here is where mnemonic, peg-word system and other memory devices come into play.

9. Pause and ponder when you hit a roadblock:

If you ever come across a hard-to-chew concept while reading a book chapter, for example, it helps to spend some time to dissect the concept. This will be necessary especially if that concept is critical to understanding other concepts later in the chapter. If you are unable to crack the nut, then endeavour to seek help.

10. Take breaks:

Doing a marathon study at one go may be tedious and tiring especially after sitting down on one spot for a while especially when the chair has no comfortable cushion. To study effectively, experts recommend taking about 15-20 minutes breaks for every 50-90 minutes that you spend studying[2]. Get up for a stretch to grab some snacks or take a walk while you recall and reflect on what you've absorbed or just cast your mind on something relaxing.

11. Test your understanding at the end:

Look for a way to assess what you've just assimilated. If you are reading a chapter in a textbook, then go over sample questions at the end of the chapter; most textbooks will have these. However, if you don't have access to any sample questions, then you can come up with your own questions or approach your prof to have your brain picked. Testing your understanding of what you have just digested actually stimulates learning and recalling of important information, and hence, gets you fired up for exams.

12. Teach it:

If you can't teach others what you've just taken in, then you probably haven't got it yet. Here is where a study group can be very helpful. It is usually great to be involved in a study group where its members share and learn from one another. A study group will likely benefit you more when your group members are at least as smart as you are. Remember two or more heads are better than one.

Writing an effective paper

Irrespective of your program, it is almost impossible to go to college or university without having to write an academic essay or paper in at least one of your courses. The task of writing a paper may be daunting at first, but once you know its benefits and learn the steps involved, you won't dread it that much. In the course of writing a paper, you'll get to hone your writing skill which will prove useful in the future at a job or a graduate program or just about anywhere else. Apart from that, writing in itself sharpens your creativity and analytical skills; after digesting a bunch of papers and synthesizing the ideas of others, you are in an excellent position to come up with your own ideas.

Allow me to walk you through steps to follow when tackling a writing assignment, tips for producing a masterpiece, and how you can improve your writing skill.

Steps in writing an effective paper
Let's suppose a sample essay question:

In Katherine Mansfield's "The Doll's House" and Guy de Maupassant's "The Necklace," discuss the dichotomy of the real versus the fake. (Word count: 1000 words.) Referencing secondary sources isn't allowed. Text: Broadview Anthology of Short Fiction Ed: 0

` Using that essay topic as an example, here are steps to follow in producing the essay:

1. Understand the task:

Spend some time finding out exactly what you've been asked to write on. Figure out what the aim of the assignment is. Is the aim to: compare and contrast, analyze and discuss, examine and investigate, or argue and persuade? Consult with the professor to make clarifications when in doubt and don't make any assumptions. Remember, if you don't know exactly what is expected of you, you'll likely not produce the right result.

Also, some writing assignments may require that no secondary sources be referenced, meaning that all ideas must be initially yours. The reason this appears to make sense is that the main aim of writing, in general, is to get you to originate your own ideas after analyzing the given texts. Thus, find out what the rules of the assignment are (for example, secondary sources permitted or not) and stick to them.

From the sample essay question, it makes sense to analyze and discuss the dichotomy of the real versus the fake in the two stories while pointing out any similarities in both stories.

2. Develop the thesis statement:

Once you are sure about the requirements of the task, with the essay question in mind, thoroughly study the texts (i.e. the primary sources and secondary sources, if applicable) and create a thesis, the main theme of the essay. The thesis statement will inform the reader of the central topic or theme, elements with which the central topic will be explained, and why what's discussed is relevant to the essay question.

Here is a possible thesis for the sample essay question:

> In "The Doll's House", this dichotomy of real versus fake is encapsulated in the relationship between the buttercup plants and the doll's house, whereas in

"The Necklace", Maupassant contrasts the two through the diamond necklace versus the pearl necklace, the Venetian cross and the roses that are rejected by Madam Loisel.

3. **Organize the materials to form an outline**:

Apply the divide-and-conquer technique by breaking down the essay into smaller parts with the aid of an outline. Brainstorm to identify the main points with corresponding supporting points, where each main point will make up one paragraph. In a nutshell, the outline should give a skeleton of the final result of the essay, having the introduction, which includes the thesis and the main points, making up about 3-5 paragraphs.

Sample outline:

Thesis: In "The Doll's House", the dichotomy of the real versus the fake is encapsulated in the relationship between the buttercup plants and the doll's house, whereas in "The Necklace", Maupassant contrasts the two through the diamond necklace versus the pearl necklace, the Venetian cross and the roses that are rejected by Madam Loisel.

Paragraph 1: The characters drew a lot of social attention to themselves, all through the images of the dollhouse and the diamond necklace.

Supporting points:
1. The dollhouse brought attention to the Burnell children at school.
2. The diamond necklace cast the spotlight on Madame Loisel at the dinner party.

Paragraph 2: The images of the necklace and the doll's house describe the characters' desire for people of their own class.

Supporting points:
1. The Burnells parents allowed only the rich kids to view the

79

dollhouse.

2. Madame Loisel being high-minded often got caught up in imagining about wealth.

Paragraph 3: The characters' fondness for artificial and superficial things is contrasted by their disregard of nature.
Supporting points:

1. At one time, the Burnell children brushed through buttercup plants in disregard, but they'd never do that to their dollhouse.

2. The Burnell children were very captivated by the painting of the dollhouse; paintings hide the real view of a thing.

3. The Kelveys were mentioned to have placed their heads inside buttercup plants, showing appreciation for nature.

4. Only the Kelveys children noticed the lamp, an element of nature/real, inside the dollhouse.

5. Madame Loisel selects a diamond necklace over a pearl necklace and a Venetian cross of gold and jewel, choosing fake/artificial over real/natural. She also refused to adorn herself with a rose flower.

That is only a simple outline. A complex one will probably have more than 3 paragraphs and may have subtopics as well.

4. Start writing:

With the outline in front of you, you can go ahead to elaborate on the significant points (one paragraph for each), providing supporting points and evidence to back up each of them. The paragraph structure should resemble the following: an introduction of the main point to be discussed, signalling the beginning of a new point; some evidence to prove the main point, then a restatement of the point.

5. **Proofread and edit**: Read the essay at least 5 times line-by-line, correcting any typing, punctuation, and grammatical errors. Do this until you are sure all mistakes have been blotted out, at least from your own point of view.

Keys to producing a masterpiece

Producing a masterpiece never happens by chance; it requires the execution of a couple of activities including:

1. **Start early**:

    Starting early will be beneficial to you especially if you give yourself enough time to get clarifications from the professor or TA regarding the essay, generate ideas, and decide which ideas are significant and which aren't. Also, in the event that you need to change your thesis, order a book or an article from a bookstore or a library outside your school. If you find yourself in a situation like this, time won't be on your side if you don't start early enough to work on the essay.

2. **Use reliable and respected sources**:

    When sourcing for materials for your essay or assignment, look out for scholarly papers, peer-reviewed journals and books by reputable individuals or organizations in the related field. Make sure to visit the school library, as it houses typically a huge wealth of writing resources that can benefit you.

3. **Make the introductory and closing paragraphs catchy**:

    The introductory paragraph shouldn't just present the thesis; it should create the context for your paper, and also capture and maintain the reader's attention. Likewise, the closing paragraph should recap the main points with the thesis and keep the reader thinking about the essay. Don't demolish the building of arguments you've constructed in the previous paragraphs by introducing a new or contradicting idea in the closing paragraph.

4. Beware of irrelevant ideas:

In an attempt to hurriedly reach the word or page count for the essay, don't get tempted to include random ideas. Keep in mind that it is not in the length of words used but in the amount of sense made. Before including any idea, ask yourself this one question - "Is this idea in any way connected to the thesis?" If the answer is yes, then you can surely welcome it to the pages of your essay, otherwise discard it and focus on another one.

5. Cite your sources:

When introducing borrowed ideas into your essay either by the use of a quotation or a paraphrase, it is recommended that you include a citation. Quotations emphasize authority and are expected to be cited when you have used more than 3 consecutive words from a source. On the other hand, use paraphrases when summarizing facts that don't require you to quote the author word-for-word. Find out from the professor which citation style is required - MLA, APA, Chicago, and so forth.

6. Have your essay reviewed thoroughly:

After reviewing the essay in your mind, take some time to read it out loud to yourself or to your friend or roommate before you hand it in. Because of the mental shortcuts adopted by the brain, you could get deceived into thinking that the essay is perfect until you hear what it sounds like. Furthermore, have tutors at the peer-review or writing centre review your work as well since they usually have a lot of writing experience.

7. **Take a break from the essay**:

Set aside about 1 to 2 days when you won't visit your essay (that is after you've completed it though). Afterward, review it a few more times. Doing this will give you a fresh view of your work and will possibly open your eyes to certain mistakes that had previously eluded you. Professional writers adopt this approach, and for sure it will work wonders for you.

8. **Give it your best shot**:

Anything worth doing is worth doing well. Once you are sure about what you are to write, put in all the effort needed to produce your best work ever. Essays usually account for a reasonable percentage of the overall course grade (about 15% or more), so put in your best to get the most marks for them – the outcome is always rewarding.

Get better at writing essays

To get better at any art, regular practice is vital. When it comes to writing essays, the same is true. Here are some tips that will help you improve your writing skills (these tips apply primarily to students whose program requires them to do a lot of writing):

1. **Read essays and articles written by other people**:

The more materials you read and the wider the subject areas you read about, the broader your vocabulary and, hence, the better your essays. When reading write-ups composed by other people, look out for the writing styles and techniques adopted, the manner of presentation of arguments and how persuasive those arguments are. If you find anything impressive, learn them and then seize opportunities to apply what you've learnt to your own essays.

2. Expand your vocabulary:

In the course of reading articles, essays or even newspapers, you'll likely come across new words you've never seen or heard before. When that happens, it helps to look up the unfamiliar words in the dictionary while observing the context in which they were used. Afterwards, jot down the new words together with their meaning in a vocabulary book that you can refer to regularly. Doing this will help you remember those words for when you need to use them in your essays. Growing your vocabulary will enable you to spice up your essays as you make the right word choices.

3. Pay attention to words structure:

There are thousands upon thousands of words in English, many of which you haven't seen or heard, so you likely don't know what they mean. The exciting thing is that there are some words whose meaning you don't necessarily have to learn only by looking them up in the dictionary. By merely seeing or hearing such words, you could guess their meanings if you are familiar with prefixes, suffixes and roots, and you understand the context in which the words are used.

Prefixes are basically words or letters added at the beginning of a word; hence, changing the word's meaning. For example, 'anti' is a prefix that means 'against' or 'opposed to'; it is found in words such as antisocial (not social), anticlockwise (going against the direction that a clock would normally go), and so forth. Suffices unlike prefixes are added at the end of a word. A common suffix is the word 'less', meaning 'without' as in ruthless (no pity or without pity), breathless (without breath), and so forth. Word root refers to the primary word to which a prefix or suffix is added.

With a good understanding of prefixes and suffixes, you can guess correctly the meaning of some new words.

4. **Use proper punctuation, writing style, syntax and voice tone**: Punctuations, when wrongly used, can change the meaning of a sentence. Therefore, be sure to apply them correctly to make it easy for the reader. Also, use different types of sentence structures to enrich your writing and to keep the reader engaged. Furthermore, as much as possible, use the active voice over the passive voice. For example, instead of writing, "Five slices of bread were eaten by me for breakfast" (which sounds a bit awkward), it would sound better to write, "I had five slices of bread for breakfast" (now that's more like it). That's passive versus active voice for you.

5. **Write, write, and write**:
One sure way to get better at anything is just to do it. To get better at writing, you have to write regularly. Elbert Hubbard, one of America's most productive writers in history once advised, "The only way to learn to write is to write and write and write and write, and write and write and write." One right way to follow through with this is by blogging (you can create your own blog site for this) or writing articles (the editorial team at your school can be a good place to start). Another way to improve is to keep a journal or diary. Maintaining a diary isn't just meant to help you recall past events; it is also a great way to express your thoughts and feelings clearly, and as you get better at that, you'll definitely improve the quality of your writing.

If you enjoy writing and will love to pursue a career in it, I highly recommend that you get a copy of the book, "The Elements of Style" by William Strunk Jr. and E.B. White. The insights provided in the book are valuable.

Acing that exam

The mention of the word alone is capable of sending shivers down students' spines. In some cases, it keeps them so nervous that they abstain from food as well as games. To worsen the case, students can't escape it if they want to graduate, at least. Surely you know what it is by now; it is nothing but – exams (yes, that's right!). You are not alone if you usually don't feel excited about exams, quizzes, or tests; even 'A+' students are not immune to the same feeling. You may be unable to entirely avoid the exam anxiety that hits you from time to time, but you can learn to boost your confidence in spite of the anxiety by efficiently preparing for the exam.

Next, I'll give you reliable and proven tips to follow before, during and after an exam so you can ace it as the 'A+' students do.

Before the exam

1. **Start preparing early**:

   To really be at your best for an exam, it's ideal that you begin preparing no later than a week before the exam. (Having a semester schedule will be very useful here. See Chapter 4 for more on a semester schedule.) The reason is that you want to give yourself enough time to create an exam study plan (basically what you are to cover and when to cover them) and to properly break down the required readings or revisions over a period of time. Trying to do the entire work just one or two days before the exam may be very hectic and stressful; hence, your chances of acing the exam may be hampered.

2. **Find out the exam coverage and format**:

   I have heard it said several times that students who do really well in exams are those who are familiar with the format and coverage of the exam and not necessarily those who are smart. Honestly speaking, there is a lot of truth in this. You need to be aware of what materials will be covered on an exam (for example, chapters 1-3 of the course text) as well as the exam format (i.e. short answers, multiple choice, True or False, essays, etc.). This knowledge will help you focus your energy, clear your doubts and build your confidence as you prepare for an exam.

3. **Revise lecture slides, class notes, and previous assignments**: If it is not the first exam for a course, you may have figured out which is the prof's focus for exam questions – lecture slides, previous assignments, course textbook, or all three. Well, whether it is the first or not, it helps to go over the lecture slides, class notes, textbook, and past assignments as questions that appear on those are testable on an exam. Profs don't waste their time preparing lecture slides or assignment questions; they have a purpose for creating those. As you review the lecture slides, pay close attention to concepts that the prof emphasized on during the lecture as those are significant clues for exam questions.

    Also, ensure to answer any unanswered questions on the lecture slides. For example, say, on the slides for a particular lecture the prof provided two problems, and he or she only supplied the solution to one of the problems. Be sure you are able to solve both the unsolved problem as well as the solved one. Furthermore, the prof may want to test students' understanding of concepts covered in past assignments, so it helps to review past assignments as well. Here is another good reason why you should do all your assignments.

4. **Go over sample exam questions**:
    Visiting sample exam questions is a great way to prepare for an exam, and you can't go wrong doing this. These sample

questions can be those provided in the course textbook at the end of each chapter, those supplied by the prof, or the ones you came up with yourself (just don't cheat yourself). In fact, the more sample questions you attempt, the more confident you'll be about the main exam, and the higher your chances of acing the exam; that's if you get your hands on the right sample questions.

5. **Be sure to understand key concepts and remember important facts**:

Exams test how good you are at grasping concepts you've been taught and at recalling important information. Therefore, endeavour to have a solid understanding of the main concepts discussed within the coverage of the exam. In some cases, you may have to memorize some important dates (for that History exam), theorems, logic and formulae (for that Math or Calculus exam), or diagrams (for that Chemistry or Biology exam).

6. **Make use of office hours**:

Since they are always willing to assist students, most profs usually make themselves more available to students especially days before exams; they are more than happy to help clarify students' doubts about the course materials. So, endeavour to maximize the profs' office hours. The same applies to the TAs and Gas.

7. **Show up for the review session**:

In the kindness of their hearts, some profs take the time to organize review session(s) prior to the exam to ensure that students are really prepared for the exam. It will do you much good to be present at such session(s) since the prof could give out hints and relevant information regarding the exam. (I am not sure you know, but some profs tend actually to create the exam questions a day before the exam; a more reason you should be at the review session.)

8. Get enough rest:

For an early morning exam, trust me you don't want to wake up feeling weak and uneasy on the morning of the exam due to insufficient rest the night before. Therefore, make sure you sleep well the night before. You need to make a conscious effort to cool down your blazing brain, so it doesn't blow a fuse during the exam. I understand that sleeping may be difficult because of exam anxiety; but please find a way to trick yourself to sleep either by playing a lullaby or turning off the lights in your bedroom or whatever works for you just so you can rest well before the exam. Whatever you do, before reposing, SET AN ALARM! There is nothing as saddening and frustrating as sleeping in all through an exam (writing the exam in your dream isn't fun at all).

9. Handle the exam anxiety:

Practice positive affirmation and visualization to shake off the fear. Each time the exam anxiety attacks declare words like - "I am not afraid of the exam; I will ace it." Or "I can do this!" Or something else you devise that will help boost your confidence. Repeat those words out loud to your hearing and watch your anxiety calm down. Motivational speakers actually recommend this as a viable strategy for combating anxiety. Besides that, visualize yourself acing the exam and leaving the exam hall smiling with confidence upon conquering the exam. Feed your mind with the images that you expect. These activities will help you maintain a positive mental attitude towards the exam, keeping your nerves down so you can concentrate on your preparation for the exam.

10. Get your tools ready:

Make sure you have the following prepared: pen, pencils, and eraser with at least one spare of each, a calculator (if allowed and required; for example for a Math exam), student ID card, and any other required item as instructed by the prof.

11. Have something to eat:

You may experience that butterfly feeling in your stomach and decide to starve because of the exam anxiety. However, try not to go into the exam on a completely empty stomach as this may affect your concentration level during the exam. Having a cup of coffee or tea with bagel or bread should do; good sources of carbs, glucose and protein are suggested.

12. Warm up your body, if you may:

For early morning exams, doing some exercise isn't a bad idea at all since it stimulates the flow of endorphins that get you feeling active and alert; a good state to be in during the exam. Some push-ups and sit-ups at home will do as well as a brisk walk to the exam hall.

During the exam (play game!)

Here are some basic and general considerations to keep in mind when taking an exam:

1. Arrive early to the exam hall:

Show up for the exam at least 15-20 minutes before the scheduled time. This will allow some time for you to calm your nerves as you say your last prayers or to exchange encouraging words with your colleagues. Rushing frantically into the exam hall some minutes late isn't a good way to begin an exam.

2. Choose a distraction-free spot:

If you have the option to choose where to sit, go for a sitting area that's far away from the windows and doors to avoid distraction.

3. Listen attentively to announcements and instructions:

Pay attention to important announcements made by the prof or proctor. The information communicated can range from the correction to a typo or missing text on the exam paper, a reminder of how much time is remaining, direction on how best to attack a complicated problem, or warning about a trick question. Keep your ears on alert.

4. Browse through the exam questions first:

After you've been asked to start the exam, don't immediately launch an attack on question one. Take the first few minutes to read the instructions and rules of the exam carefully. Afterwards, for short answers questions especially, quickly run through the entire exam questions, so you know how to allot time to each question, paying close attention to how much marks each question is worth. Scanning through the entire exam questions first actually sets your mind to work on retrieving solutions to other problems while you are working on a different question. When you do this, you'll be surprised by how quickly you are able to recall relevant information and come up with solutions during the exam; it isn't magic but just your mind at work.

5. **Read the questions carefully and closely:**

   Don't be in haste when reading a question. Read each question entirely at least once to fully understand it before providing an answer. If you need any clarifications, don't hesitate to ask the proctor immediately.

6. **Focus on higher-value questions:**

   Different questions on an exam are worth different scores. Therefore, look out for questions that are allotted higher scores and spend enough time to complete them. It is better to correctly complete a question that weighs 30% than to complete three questions that all account for 15% of the overall exam score. (And for sure, it is even much better to complete all questions still.)

7. **Attempt all questions:**

   Unless you'll be penalized for providing a wrong answer, endeavour to answer all questions based on what you know. You may get partial marks for providing an incorrect solution (this applies to short answer questions), but you'll definitely receive no mark if you provide no response. Apart from that, it breaks the heart of some profs to see questions left unanswered when they are marking the exam papers. That's probably why most of them encourage students to attempt all questions.

8. **Don't panic when you hit rocky questions:**

   It may so happen that you're easily and progressively knocking off the soft exam questions, but suddenly you hit a tough one; the first response may be to sleep on that question and eventually break down, which shouldn't be so. Whenever you encounter a difficult question, instead of spending the rest of your time on it, mark it and move onto another question. Revisit the hard question(s) after completing all the other not-so-hard questions.

9. **Review, review, review:**

Personally, I can't overemphasize how helpful it is to review answer sheets even after completing the exam. It is a grade saver. Take time to go over your solutions to ensure that all the steps and the final answers are correct. Revisit each question to make sure you've selected the right answer for each and that no question was omitted. Do this over and over again until you are 100% sure that your answers are accurate and your answer sheet is ready to hit the prof's desk for an 'A+.'

10. **Use up the entire exam time:**

Once you submit your answer sheet and leave the exam hall, that's the end of the exam for you; you won't be allowed to make any more changes to your answers. For this reason, it is suggested that you exhaust all the time permitted you for an exam except you have to leave to finalize your preparation for another exam or to handle something else that's urgent and important. Don't ever get intimidated by students who leave the exam hall in the first 15 or 25 minutes; the truth is that some students actually submit full or half blank answer sheets (I was shaken from my root when I first heard about this). Always remember that it's your grades you are concerned about here and not someone else's. So, review your work till the end of the exam even if you are the only one left in the hall; others may think you to be dumb when you do this, but the grades will tell later.

11. Get set for the next one or go fizzle out the stress:

Once you are done with the exam, you should go relax and rest if you don't have any exams left to write soon - you deserve it. Otherwise, go finalize your preparation for any upcoming exams - you need it.

Now let's see some tips specific to the different exam formats - multiple choices and short answers:

Multiple choice tests

1. Pay attention to modifiers:

Watch out for words such as "except", "all", "not", and so forth. For example, you may come across a question that reads: "All are names of the nine planets **except** one." In haste or excitement, you may select "All of the above" if that is one of the options or some other wrong option simply because you subconsciously ignored the word "except" even though it was typed in bold print. It happens. Also, a question may ask for the "most appropriate" or "best" answer which means that 1 or more options are accurate, but the most accurate one is the right answer. Just watch out for those modifiers.

2. Don't linger over one question:

Since each question on a multiple choice exam almost always weighs the same point, you can skip a tough question then revisit it after completing the other questions. This helps to keep the momentum going.

3. Answer all questions:

Try not to leave any question unanswered especially if you won't get penalized for supplying an incorrect answer. In the worst case you'll get it wrong, but then in the best case, you'll get it right.

4. Check that you have the right circles shaded:

When shading an answer on the scantron form, ensure that it matches the right question. For example, don't make the mistake of selecting option 'C' for question 3 when answering question 2; doing this can cause a brutal wrong-answer domino effect on your scantron form. To avoid this disaster, you can place a blank sheet of paper over the unanswered questions, uncovering them as you move down the scantron form to provide your answer.

5. Don't rely on patterns:

Maybe you've noticed that in some multiple choice exams, patterns seem to emerge on the scantron form. For example, the correct answer for questions 1-10 could be 'B' then 'D' for questions 15 – 20. The prof may not have done that intentionally and apparently won't want to leave such an easy clue for students. So, don't depend on such emerging patterns for the right answers; instead, trust your knowledge and intuition.

6. Catch the clue for 'All of the above':

Some questions normally have the option, "All of the above" and should be answered with caution. However, here is one thing to consider for such questions: if you are 100% sure that 2 or more options are correct and only one answer is to be picked, then the right answer for that question should be - 'All of the above.'

7. Apply the option elimination rule:

Each question will have about 4 or 5 options of which one is the correct answer while the rest are wrong. Thus, if you are having a hard time deciding which is the correct answer, you can go on to mark off the wrong answers, one by one. Eventually, you'll be left with the last option standing – the correct one.

Short-answer or problem-solving type tests

1. **Responses should be on point**:

   When responding to short answer or problem-solving type questions, the strategy is different. If you are asked for a definition, give a definition. If you are asked to list only 5 items, list the 5 only not 10 (there will probably be no extra mark for going the extra mile here). However, when asked for an explanation, which is quite a different case, feel free to supplement the explanation with a diagram to demonstrate your solid understanding of the question.

2. **Show all workings**:

   For courses such as Calculus, Math or Physics where calculations are required, it helps to show all the steps that led to the final answer. In most cases, even though your final answer is wrong, you could still receive partial marks for showing your workings.

3. **Make no assumptions**:

   If you aren't sure about a question, instead of working solely based on your own assumptions, get clarification and confirmation from the prof or proctor.

4. **Write legibly**:

   Make sure your handwriting is clear enough for the grader to see. If the grader can't see something you've written, don't expect him or her to go looking for you to get clarification; marking piles of exam papers is already enough pain so the grader may not even bother looking for you. To this end, before submitting your answer sheet, double-check with the prof or proctor that your handwriting is legible.

After the exam

Irrespective of your performance on an exam, don't take it personally especially if you've just bombed it. Your grade on an exam isn't a real reflection of your intelligence or identity. It probably demonstrates your readiness for the exam, and hopefully, you'll do better as you get more prepared for subsequent exams. Having said that, here are some things to do after an exam:

1. **Go over your graded exam**:

    Never miss an opportunity to go over your exam after it has been graded. Doing this may be unpleasant at times, but it is worth the effort especially if you plan to perform better on subsequent exams. There are two main reasons you want to do this though. For one, questions on an exam (for example, first or second term exam) may reappear on the final exam (maybe not exact questions but similar) because in most cases exams cover the entire semester's work. Thus, if you fail to learn from your mistakes on a particular exam, you'll likely repeat the same mistakes on the final. Secondly, it hurts not to know what you don't know since you can't improve on something you are unaware of. Remember, you are committed to a lifestyle of learning, part of which requires that you learn about what you know little or nothing of, so you can improve on it.

2. **Don't miss the review/correction session**:

    Usually, on the next lecture after the exam, the prof will talk about the results of the exam and possibly return the exam scripts back to the students. After that, the prof reviews the exam questions and supplies the ideal answers to those. This is a great time to learn so you can do better on the next exam.

3. **Meet with the prof in case of any complaints**:

    If after looking through your graded exam paper you feel you deserve more marks for a question or two, then don't hesitate to approach your professor. One thing though, be polite when you meet with the professor to discuss concerns about your grade; don't burst into his or her office demanding a grade boost as you'd likely not get it this way. Even if you don't receive the extra marks you were hoping for, still find out from the prof what you did wrong and what you could do to get a better grade moving forward.

4. **Apply the zero-based thinking approach**:

    Once you have admitted your mistakes on the exam, it is time to apply the zero-based thinking technique. Basically, it says that knowing what you know now, what would you do differently if you have to start things over again? When applied to exams, it will read something like this: based on what you've learnt from your errors on the recent exam, what will you do differently on the next exams? Here are some examples to help you:

    a. "I didn't finish up the exam, so on the next exam I'll budget my time efficiently and not linger over a single question."

    b. "I made ridiculous mistakes, so on the next exam I'll make sure to review my answer sheet a couple more times before submitting."

    c. "I received a half mark on a question because I didn't show my working. Going forward, I'll have to show all my working on my exams."

    d. "I got so thirsty and uncomfortable that I had to leave the exam hall to buy a bottle of water; I lost some time doing this. Henceforth, I'll always carry a bottle of water along with me to the exam hall exam."

You get the idea – right? Take some time to agree on what you'll do differently considering the errors you committed on the most recent exams.

With the tips and guides spelt out here, you'll be well on your way to preparing optimally for and acing upcoming exams.

Delivering a powerful presentation

Scared of public speaking? You aren't alone. There are many successful people today who, at early stages in their life, battled with the fear of public speaking. One good example is Warren Buffet, one of the wealthiest men in the world currently. In college, Mr. Buffett avoided courses that required presentations. In fact, at one time after he had registered for a public speaking course, he soon chickened out from it even before the course commenced. However, seeing the unequalled benefits of being a good communicator, Mr. Buffett finally enrolled in a public speaking class. He later developed effective communication and presentation skills which he labelled as being foundational to his success in life.[3]

Similar experiences were encountered by some of the most successful spiritual, business and technical leaders and speakers in our time. In most of the cases out there, it is clear that to overcome the fear of public speaking, i.e. glossophobia, those individuals had to: acknowledge that fear, maintain a positive attitude toward it, and push themselves to overcome the fear by just doing the same fear-causing activity. These are sure steps to vanquish the fear of public speaking, and I too can testify to that.

Maybe you've just enrolled in a course that requires you to give presentations, or you plan to enrol in such a course, but you are not sure how you'll cope. No need to worry because by sticking to the following tips, you'll be on your way to delivering a compelling and captivating presentation.

1. Know your audience:

Yes, it is your talk, but then it is not just about you because your audience matters equally. Communication is not complete until the speaker's message has been well received by the listeners (i.e. your audience). In order for this to happen, you should at least have some basic knowledge about your audience; this knowledge can range from their level of education or understanding of the presentation topic, their major, and other information you feel may impact the content of your talk. The more you know about your audience, the higher your chances of using appropriate vocabulary and examples to communicate effectively with them. This way, your audience will benefit from your presentation to a larger extent.

2. Do your research:

One of the main reasons students fumble on presentations is that they haven't properly researched and organized the materials for their talk. Lack of confidence in the content of one's talk is enough to awaken the fear of bombing the presentation. That said, keep on with your homework till you are confident about what you've gathered. In addition, if the choice of the talk depends on you, then pick a topic that you are interested in and passionate about because then you are more apt to perform well. On the other hand, if you are just thrown some random topic, then you'll probably have to spend more time doing research (the topic may not be that bad at all).

3. Practice, practice, practice:

Nothing can take the place of practice when preparing for a

presentation (except you are as great a speaker as Dr. Martin Luther King Jr.). In his program, *How to Prepare a Powerful Presentation*, professional speaker and author, Brian Tracy remarked, "If you plan and prepare and organize an excellent talk, you will have done the heavy lifting." According to him, preparation is about 90% of the work. There is no better way to prepare for your presentation than practice.

When practicing for your presentation, it helps to try it out before a friend or a family member so you can get instant feedback on your performance. If, however, you don't find someone to play the audience, you can record yourself with your smartphone or video camera if you have one. Watch yourself in the recording and be the judge (this can feel really weird at times). Actually, I suggest that you practice at the exact location of the main presentation if you can; this way you'll familiarize yourself with the environment. Also, it is a good idea to time yourself while you practice, so you don't overshoot the time allotted you; good speakers stick to the time allotted them.

4. Apply creative visualization:

Practicing your presentation physically is great, but when you combine that with the mental practice through visualization, the result is phenomenal. The mental practice is an extension of the physical one only that it can be done anywhere and anytime. Basically, take time to play the presentation in your mind over and over again while on your bed, on the transit commuting to school or back home, and just about wherever possible. As you do this, imagine yourself at your best, delivering the presentation like a pro and using appropriate gestures as you engage with the audience; the result of this mental rehearsal is a series of small wins in the stage of your mind which will culminate to the big victory on the physical stage. In short, carrying out creative visualization in this area will help build your confidence as you get set for your presentation.

5. Calm down and speak slowly:

Never yield to the temptation of slurring your words like a rapper so you can quickly complete your presentation and leave the stage; that's not a good idea. Always maintain your calm and speak slowly so that your audience can follow through with your talk from the start till the end. Apart from that, calming down and speaking slowly can help with breath control especially when you are nervous.

6. Maintain good posture:

When you present yourself before the audience, stand straight with your head lifted up and your arms suspended beside you. Avoid crossing your arms in front of you or standing with arms akimbo as both may appear threatening to your audience.[4] Just be yourself, and you'll be fine.

7. Engage with the audience:

Remember that you are speaking to the audience and not just throwing words at them. Therefore, it is always a good idea to maintain eye contact with individuals in the audience. (Just imagine having a conversation with someone and all through the talk the person didn't look you in the eyes; how would you feel?) You can start off by looking at the friendly faces in the room as those are encouraging. If you'll get discouraged easily by looking at certain individuals, who are dozing off, tapping their cell phones, or staring back at you in an unfriendly manner, then try not to look at such individuals again.

Irrespective of the reactions of the audience, allow your mind to remain on your talk and not on the audience. Don't take any of those reactions personally. Besides that, when necessary, feel free to use an appropriate hand, arm or head gestures when explaining or emphasizing main points. However, be careful not to distract your audience by shifting their focus from your presentation to, say, your chain wristwatch that tinkles whenever you jerk your hand, for example.

8. **Start with an attention-grabbing opening**:

Powerful presentations usually seize the attention of the audience right from the beginning. This effect can be achieved by employing attention-getters such as anecdotes, rhetorical questions, quotes, statements of benefit, all of which should be related to the topic of the talk. For example, suppose that you are giving a presentation on the power of compound interest, after introducing the topic, you can say something like this:

"By the end of this presentation, you'll learn how you can have more than enough money to enable you to live your ideal life after retirement by applying the power of compound interest."

Make a good first impression with a powerful opening as you set the stage for your main points.

9. **Use effective connectors to link your main points**:

Just as you would do when writing a paper, use logical connectors to indicate a transition from one main point to the other. Such connectors include: "Moving on…", "Next…", "Last but not the least…" or the sequences - "First…", "Second…", "Third…", or "One…", "Two…", "Three…" (Supposing that you have three main points to discuss). Furthermore, just as with a paper, follow the same structure when discussing your main points: state the point, present supporting evidence, then restate the point just as a reminder.

10. Give a memorable closing:

Effective presentations usually leave the audience asking for more especially with an effective closing. Similar to the opening, you can end the presentation with a call for action, a motivational quote, or a story. For example, suppose that you are delivering a speech on the power of positive thinking, you can end your presentation like this:

> "Just as Napoleon Hill once wrote, 'Whatever the mind can conceive and believe it can achieve.' I believe that you can achieve just about anything you commit to accomplish, remembering that if you can think it, you can do it."

To get some motivation on public speaking, you can check out the famous "I have a dream" speech by Martin Luther King Jr. (You'll literally get pumped up.)

Handling that big project

You probably are familiar with dealing with individual projects and assignments which are one-man jobs. In college and university, times will come when you have to face complex projects which will require more than your two strong hands and one big brain to get the work completed well and on time. In fact, in the real world, complex projects are seldom done by one person but by a group of people, so taking part in group projects at school presents you with a glimpse of this future.

Working in a group creates a forum for you to develop

interpersonal, teamwork, and leadership skills. It is also a great way to identify your strengths and weaknesses and to apply your skills to solve real problems.[5] These are only a few benefits working in a group offers and I believe that as you get involved in group projects, you'll appreciate the values that it provides.

Still worried about working in a group? Have your group follow these tips and watch that anxiety fall away:

1. **Have a proper first-time group meet-up**:

   Once the group members are known, it's a good idea to have the group meet up to mingle. The members should get to know one another well enough at least to the extent that each person is comfortable working with one another. The group has to be reminded of the reason for its formation which is to complete a complex project, the expectations of each member, and the deadlines and sub-deadlines for the project.

2. **Agree on a means of communication**:

   If possible, during the first meeting, the group should decide on the most preferred means of communication, be it email, telephone, Facebook, or whatever it may be. The better the flow and quality of communication within the group, the better the collaboration and, hence, the higher the chances of getting the work done well and on time.

3. **Every member is a leader**:

   To avoid conflicts especially where one group member tries to boss his or her way in the group activities, the leadership hat should be rotated around the group members. This will also give everyone in the group the opportunity to develop their leadership skills. Just so it is clear, taking the leadership role doesn't mean that one is to complete all the tasks; the leader is meant to coordinate and delegate the group tasks, ensure that the tasks are distributed fairly amongst the members and track the group's progress on the project.

4. **Get to work as soon as possible**:

Some group activities may require a couple of trials-and-errors; so once the main goal or task has been identified, the group is to begin brainstorming right away to decide on the final action plan that actually works. Once that is decided, get to work immediately.

5. **Task should be assigned specifically and individually**:

To eliminate social loafing in the team, every member should be encouraged to participate in the project. One way to make this happen is to have the tasks assigned to each member based on his or her strengths and skills set. Then after each meeting, it helps to have a reminder sent to the group based on the means of communication agreed on by the group. The reminder should state the meeting summary, what tasks each person was assigned, and the expected deadlines. This way no one can give the common excuse - "I didn't know I was to work on that."

6. **Be prepared to do extra tasks**:

Sometimes things don't turn out as expected; a group member may stop showing up to lectures and meetings, or you may get thrown into the "wrong" group. Irrespective of the case, you have no choice than to go the extra mile to fill in the gaps because you care to save your grades (I know you really do).

A friend of mine in a college shared an unpleasant experience she once had while working on a group project. Apparently, she got assigned to a group where she was the only English native,

(English was the language of instruction in the school); the other members of the group weren't English natives, so they struggled to speak and write in English. It was a hard time for her as she had to find a way to translate between two languages during the group meetings. To make matters worse, one by one her group members began to disappear from the lectures and group meetings, leaving her to do all the presentations and reports alone. The end result? My friend pulled through the challenge because she was determined to excel.

As you plan for the best on your group project and hope things go as planned (knock on wood), be ready to do some extra work just in case things spin off tangent.

7. **Attack the problem, not the person**:

Whenever two or more people come together for a common purpose, conflicts usually are not rare. If (or when) a member of the group is beginning to act irresponsibly – consistently missing group meetings, not completing tasks by the deadline or not doing the tasks at all – it is probably not a good idea for the rest of the group to immediately pounce on the erring member as that may only aggravate matters. The group can start off by finding out why that one member is acting differently. The person may be going through some personal or family struggle and may need some help. Understanding members' challenges will help provide the right kind of support and encouragement needed.

On the other hand, if the erring member is just trying to be a pain in the neck, the group should remind the individual of how his or her behaviour may jeopardize the group's performance. If the individual fails to change, then the group should take actions based on whatever it agrees (e.g. give the individual a poor score on the group member evaluation at the end of the course while covering up for the person for the time being).

8. **Have different deadlines for the sub-tasks**:

   Group members could be unpredictable sometimes. To absorb any shocks, the deadlines for individual tasks (i.e. the sub-tasks) should be earlier than the actual project deadline set by the instructor. Just to be safe.

9. **Don't hesitate to consult the course instructor when necessary**:

   The course instructor probably has been teaching the course for a while and will have a good experience. Therefore, whenever the group encounters any issues involving a difficult group member or the group project itself, seek help from the instructor as he or she will be happy to help.

Putting them all together

It is time to put into practice what you've learnt about studying effectively, acing your exams, writing an effective paper, delivering a compelling presentation, and handling a group project. As you do so, you'll be paving the way to achieving your desired grades (I am already excited for you).

School life isn't just about the academic realm. It also includes the realms of health, social, extracurricular, financial (as in money management) and mental attitudes. The truth of the matter is that your academic work can be affected by these other areas. Want to learn more about maintaining a balance in all the realms of school life? The next chapter will show you that.

Roll up your sleeves

1. Make the most of your study time by considering the tips specified in "Study like an 'A' student" section in this chapter.

2. Before writing your next paper, look at the "Steps in writing an effective paper" in this chapter and see how you can apply them to your work.

3. As discussed in this chapter, one way to get better at writing is to either begin blogging, writing articles or keeping a diary; these will help you clearly express your thoughts. So, consider which one you can pick to start with if you plan to improve your writing skill. (Getting a journal seems like an easy one to start with.)

4. Before your next exam, resolve to follow the exam tips (before, during, and after) discussed in this chapter.

5. Are you interested in overcoming your fear of public speaking? If yes, then consider enrolling in a public speaking course. You'll never get worse at public speaking only better if you choose to take this bold step of faith. Apart from that, look for opportunities to develop your presentation and communication skills either by joining a communication group on campus or a teaching department at a not-for-profit organization.

6. Working in a group is very beneficial. When dealing or working with a group, resolve to follow the points listed in the section "Handling the big project" in this chapter

CHAPTER SIX

Beyond the academic realm

*"Balance is the key to everything. What we do,
think, say, eat, feel, they all require awareness,
and through awareness, we can grow"*
~~ Koi Fresco

More students are learning to balance their school life, and this is translating to them having a fulfilling time at school. The good news is that you too can be one of them. So far, we have only covered the academic path of your school journey. But then there is more to the journey than that path alone. Generally speaking, your school life comprises various areas including academic, social, extracurricular, spiritual, and so forth. Failure in one area can trickle into other areas just as success in one area is evident in the other areas. For example, if you fail to eat healthily and neglect your physical fitness, thriving on junk food only, you could fall ill and become unable to study effectively; your academic performance may suffer as a result. You may also become sluggish and unable to cope with the hectic schedule at school.

Likewise, you may lose interest in your study and get discouraged if you get broke and can't meet your basic needs. That is why you can't afford to be that nerd who coops himself in his room, reading 24/7. In most cases, he is malnourished from eating unhealthily, overweight from not exercising regularly, broke from mismanaging his funds, bored from not getting involved and pessimistic from nursing a negative mental attitude. Don't be that guy! Don't be that girl!

In this chapter, you'll learn how to get involved outside the classroom, manage your funds, eat healthy, stay fit, and maintain a positive mental attitude.

Get involved outside the classroom

You enrolled in school to get some education which will prepare you for a bright future. While the curricular activities (coursework) play a key role in your education, complementing those with both extracurricular and co-operative education (co-op) or internship programs will not only make you well-rounded but will also add extra sparkles to your bright future. It also looks good on your résumé.

Why get involved outside the classroom?

You may be wondering how you can benefit from getting involved outside the classroom. In fact, I will be glad to clear any doubts in your minds concerning that. Engaging in co-op or internship programs or other extracurricular activities, often result in the following benefits:

1. **Build up and embellish your résumé even before you graduate:**

   You don't have to (and you shouldn't) wait until after your graduation to begin entering new skills into your résumé. In fact, if you choose to do that, your plain résumé will most likely not catch the attention of most recruiters. Also, if you are just like everyone else, only paying attention to the curricular work and possessing similar skill sets and grade average as with the majority, how would you stand out amongst your peers? Gaining practical experience through co-op and internship programs as well as acquiring soft skills by participating in extracurricular activities will provide you with enough skills required to develop an eye-catching résumé. With those programs, you'll get the opportunity to apply in a real-world setting, the knowledge acquired from the classroom, as well as grow your professional network even before you graduate. The skills and experiences you acquire will distinguish you from your peers, and give you an edge in the fiercely competitive market. Furthermore, soft skills as simple as effective time management, organization, leadership and customer service skills, when demonstrated in your résumé can be the reason you are preferred over other candidates in a hiring process.

2. Make some money:

Participating in co-op and internship programs not only exposes you to practical hands-on experience but also opens for you an income opportunity. The funds you earn can be geared toward paying your bills and rent, saving for a worthy purpose, and giving yourself some required treats. What's rewarding is that when you begin handling those financial needs by yourself, you'll help relieve your parents of some burdens, and awaken in yourself a sense of independence; that in itself is a key sign of maturity.

3. Gain a sense of belonging:

We, humans, are social beings; hence, we enjoy the company of others. In Abraham Maslow's hierarchy of human needs, the sense of belonging appears on the third level of the hierarchy, suggesting its importance. Joining a student group or a sports team, for example, creates a forum for you to make new friends and to establish social connections; this will trigger a sense of belonging to you. Social psychologist and assistant professor at Stanford University, Gregory Walton, once said, "Our interests, motivation, health and happiness are inextricably tied to the feeling that we belong to a greater community that may share common interests and aspirations." Therefore, by actively participating in a group, and enjoying the feeling of belongingness, you'll be combating loneliness, homesickness and possibly depression.

4. Get insight into making better career decisions:

By partaking in co-op or internship programs, you can learn what type of work culture you prefer, determine whether or not you are in the right field, and discover your strengths and weaknesses (both professional and personal). In short, those programs can help you determine whether or not you'll enjoy the career path your current major is taking you to.

In speaking about the benefit of getting involved, career coach Alina Tubman said, "It's a great way to build your professional skills including leadership, teamwork, communication and prioritization. All these skills are necessary for students applying for jobs and internships."

Extracurricular activities

On campus, there are several extracurricular activities you can get involved in. You can join a sports team (for example, athletic team, football or basketball team, and so forth) or a student clubs (for example, Engineers Without Borders (EWB), Astronomy club, Science club, Shinerama, and so forth). If you are interested in learning a foreign language but dread taking a course for that, you can join a language club to learn the basics before you proceed to take the language course. At some schools, the International Student Office on campus organizes forums where students, both natives and non-natives of a foreign language, meet up regularly to converse in the language; this has proven to be an effective way to learn not only a foreign language but also a foreign culture. Find out about the language conversation forum at your school if you are interested in learning a new language.

In addition, the staff at the students' media (newspaper press and radio station) on campus will be happy to have you if you are outspoken and enjoy writing. Joining the media team will allow you to hone your communication skills. Furthermore, whenever the need arises, you can enhance your leadership skills by seeking executive positions at a student club or more interestingly at the student union on campus.

Opportunities for extracurricular activities outside of campus are in abundance as well; you only need to know your area(s) of interest. For example, if writing is your thing and you'd love an adventure outside of campus, you can volunteer at a local newspaper press. You can give back to the community by volunteering for outreaches and fundraising events organized by churches, charity or other not-for-profit organizations.

All I ask is that you be moderate when selecting the activities to partake in. Better to be an active member of one or two clubs than to be a passive member of ten clubs. Also, ensure that your academic work isn't neglected because of your involvement in extracurricular activities; let balance be your watchword.

Co-op and internship programs

As earlier mentioned, co-op and internship programs are great opportunities for you to gain real-world experience as you put to practice what you've learned in the classroom. In addition, you'll be receiving compensation for your work (this is true for co-op positions but not for all internship positions). In fact, depending on your school and your major, both programs may account for credits toward your degree.

Unlike extracurricular activities which in most cases may be unrelated to your career, co-op and internship programs are usually career-related. Although they have a couple of similarities, co-op and internship differ:

Co-op	Internship
Paid	Paid or unpaid
Requires completion of 2-3 work term placements which are about 4 – 16 months in total	Requires the completion of a single work term placement of 4 – 12 months
Students alternate between work and study times such that for each semester, a student is either working full-time or studying full-time.	Usually done during the summer when a student is not taking any classes.

In most cases, fees are attached to these programs, but then the returns are usually worth the extra costs.

How to increase your chances of landing a co-op or internship placement

Getting hired for a co-op or internship placement can be quite challenging especially for freshmen who have little or no prior work experience. However, that shouldn't keep you from participating in the program, seeing the benefits it has. In fact, here are some tips to help assist you with landing a co-op or an internship placement:

1. Make good use of your career advisers:

Just as you would approach your professors for help with your coursework, endeavour to consult your career advisers to guide you through the work placement process. In Chapter 2, I shared with you how supportive career advisers usually are, using my own experience which was very positive. Honestly speaking, they contributed significantly to the foundation of my career journey, and I believe they can do the same for you. Career advisers are dedicated to assisting you to attain a successful career experience, so make good use of their service.

2. Grow your network:

Since you are not in the industry yet, you want to stay abreast of the latest happenings in your field of interest. One of the best ways to do that is to garner information from those who are in the industry regularly. Your parents, relatives and friends can suggest to you the right industry's professionals to approach, or you can find them on professional networking websites, like LinkedIn. Once you have found the professional, take another step to chat with the person or more formally, interview the person. Be careful not to act on your own; guidance and caution are advised.

During informational interviews with professionals, either in person or via phone, you want to find out from the person what skills are in high demand in the market, how those can be acquired, and how you can best prepare for and thrive in the industry. As you have more of these informational interviews with different people, you'll be developing a clearer picture of the industry you'll be going into and your future career path.

Also, endeavour to attend job fairs as they offer networking opportunities with potential employers. Before walking into a job fair, be ready to deliver to employers a 60-seconds self-introductory speech and have some copies of your résumé to hand out to them. In any case, go prepared and dress professionally for success.

3. Hang on tight, don't quit:

You may not land a co-op or internship position on your first attempt, and I understand that it can be disappointing, but don't give up hope. Always remember, "Winners never quit, and quitters never win." If you ever find yourself disappointed from not being able to secure a co-op or internship position, remember to get back on your feet and explore options to acquire new skills either by taking up an unpaid position or enrolling in online courses. This way you'll be maximizing your time while preparing yourself for greater opportunities to come.

During my undergrad, my first attempt to secure a co-op placement was unsuccessful. Discouraging as it was, I didn't opt out of the co-op program even after a couple of my friends quit and tried to convince me to do the same. That summer, I registered for an online course that was related to my major, got a part-time job on campus, and joined a catering class organized at my church at that time. Fortunately, by the following semester when I sought for a co-op position, it didn't elude me because I had prepared myself for the opportunity. I obviously won't have got it had I quit the co-op program. That first job opened bigger doors for me as I moved forward.

4. Strategically plan your work-study sequence:

In some cases, it is helpful to know what period of the year you likely should and should not be applying for a co-op or internship position. For example, in the summer there will likely be a lot of candidates applying for jobs than during other periods (everyone looks forward to working in the summer). This means that freshmen (first-year folks) will be competing with seniors (say third or final year folks) who are more likely to be preferred over the former who may lack experience. So, you can plan to study during those busy periods and apply for a job at the not-so-busy periods. You may want to consider this strategy especially if you don't yet possess the skills and experience that are on demand in the job market (I understand that some freshmen may already have the required skills and experiences, but for those who don't, you should get them with time).

I know that this may not be guaranteed to work but it worked for me and some other individuals I know. Also, find out from your career advisers if you are able to change your work-study sequence.

From an editor in law school to the president of a great nation

Have you ever heard the name - Barack Obama? I am sure you have. Here is something interesting about his educational background you may not have heard about. Obama, as you may know, attended Harvard Law School. By the end of his first year, he became an editor for the Harvard Law Review which was a student group in the law school. In his second year, he was named the president of that student group. Later on, for about two years, he worked as a research assistant under a professor and scholar of liberal constitutional law, Laurence H. Tribe.

You would think that by participating in all these extracurricular activities, Obama's academic work suffered. In fact, that was very far from the case as he graduated from law school with great honours (or first class or magna cum laude as in Latin). Even before entering law school, he had been engaged in public speaking which he eventually became a master of (remember his "Yes we can" speech). He later became a professor, a senator and a president of the United States of America. What a journey!

It is evident that Obama's engagement in extracurricular activities while in school played a huge role in forming and preparing him for the position of president of the United States of America. So, don't think for a second that getting involved in extracurricular activities at school is a sheer waste of your time. Obama is just one example; there are many, many more!

Know your priorities

At college or university, you may observe that while some students tend to focus more on extracurricular activities, others focus more strictly on academic work. For example, a student, who clinched some athletic scholarships upon admission, will likely devote a significant portion of time on the field versus on coursework in order to maintain the awards (say 60% on the field and 40% on coursework). The opposite is the case for a student who is dependent on several academic scholarships; he or she may feel pressured to spend more time on coursework than on anything else (say 75% on coursework and 25% elsewhere). Based on their priorities and goals, I think students should be able to allocate their time and resources to achieve their desired end even as they balance play and work.

Likewise, it helps to be crystal-clear on what your priorities are so that you are not distracted and wrongly influenced by your friends. As a scholar, for instance, you shouldn't be comparing the number of hours you and an athletic friend spend on coursework; your hours obviously should be the higher of the two. Know your priorities and focus on them.

Manage your funds

Before now, you probably haven't had to manage your own funds all by yourself. Advancing to post-secondary education demands that you have a good grasp of the basics of money management, so you don't blow away your piggy bank. There is always something new to learn about wisely managing funds, and the more you know, the better you become at it. Your best bet is to constantly seek advice from your parents, relatives and financial advisors at the financial institution you bank with. Meanwhile, I have some tips that you can start off with.

Tips for managing your funds
1. Have a budget and track your expenses:
As a student, a budget is an extremely valuable tool that will guard you against getting broke. I recommend that you create a monthly budget and discipline yourself to stay within its bounds. Creating a budget requires that you take into account your income sources such as payment from a job, monetary gifts from relatives or friends, or parent allowances; then estimate how much you plan to spend each month on your needs and wants such as rent, bills, textbooks, outing, among others. You also want to know where your money goes, by recording every expense you incur from as little as buying a cup of Tim Horton's coffee to picking up a TV set from an electronics store. Keep the recording practice simple by using a spreadsheet, or if you are techy enough, you can get one of the free expenses recording apps (for example, Mint, Wallaby, Wally, and so forth).

Finally, by the end of each month, determine whether or not you did a good job at spending less than you earned. If you did – well done and keep up! Otherwise, I suggest that you carefully review your expense records to see which expenses can be eliminated in the coming months.

Here is a sample budget and an expenses collection for a particular month:

ITEM/SERVICE	COST ($)
Rent	330
Grocery	130
Phone bill	50
Internet bill	47.55
Miscellaneous(textbook, cloth, stationery, etc)	300
Total	**$ 857.55**

Warren's monthly budget

ITEM/SERVICE	COST ($)
Rent	330
Grocery (foodstuffs)	150
Phone bill	60.22
Internet bill	47.55
Textbook	200
Stationery	35
TOTAL	**$822.44**

Warren's expenses record for September 2012

From the sample budget and expenses collection above, it is clear that in September 2012, Warren spent less than he had budgeted for, leaving his closing balance for that month in a positive. (Good job Warren! I hope he keeps up the good work moving forward.)

There will be months when you'll spend more than you had budgeted due to some unforeseen events. When (or if) that happens don't beat yourself up and at the same time don't celebrate; revisit your expenses record and look for ways to avoid any unnecessary expenses in the coming months.

2. **Distinguish your needs from your wants**:

It is essential that you are able to differentiate between your needs and your wants. Your needs are items or services you can't do without; for example, food, clothes, shelter (accommodation), and the others; whereas your wants are items that aren't required but are good to have anyway; for example, pet dog or cat, Xbox One, etc.

To ascertain whether an item is a "need" or "want", try living without it for a few weeks and see if you can cope. If you can't then perhaps it's a "need" otherwise, it can be classified as a "want." Having knowledge of your wants will help you identify what items you can do away with to cut down on your expenses so you can save some money.

3. **Develop the habit of saving more**:

Statistics from the insurance industry once revealed that of 100 individuals who start working by age 21, 1 of them would be rich, 4 will be financially independent, 15 will have sufficient money, and the remaining 80 will be working, broke, or pension-dependent due to insufficient funds[1]. Your goal is to be rich or, at worse, to be financially independent. To achieve this goal, you want to begin now to form the habit of saving more and spending less.

By default, there seems to be in us an innate connection between happiness and spending money that stirs up an urge to gratify our immediate desires. That urge was evident in our early childhood when all we did with the coins in our piggy bank was to buy candies. The same urge drove us at adolescence to lavish our money on items we didn't need (fancy shoes and clothing - you know what I mean). But now that you have become the director of your own finances, you want to sever that link between happiness and spending money, and then reconnect happiness with saving and investing the money instead.

To assist you with this, I strongly recommend that you open a savings account (if you don't have one already) into which you deposit money at a fixed or variable interval depending on whether you have a job or not. If you hold a job, the rule of thumb is that you pay yourself first by putting aside at least 10% of your pay toward saving. If you feel 10% is too much for you, start with as little as 1% then gradually increase the percentage either monthly or quarterly as you get comfortable. Obviously, you are not exempted from saving money if you are without a job; still, endeavour to save a percentage of your allowances or gifts. One thing though, before proceeding to open your savings account, resolve to resist the temptation of withdrawing from the account except when necessary; for instance, during an emergency or when it is really needed.

Eventually, after you must have fattened your savings account, consider looking into one of the several investment options, such as stocks, bonds, mutual funds, amongst the others. Discuss with an investment advisor at your bank to discover what option suits you best. Always remember that money in the bank dispels anxiety especially in the case of emergency.

4. **Use your credit card with caution**:

When used wisely, a credit card is a great way to obtain a reputable credit history which will prove very useful when you choose to secure a loan for a mortgage, rent an apartment, or lease a car (these are most applicable to those in the Western world). As a student at college or university, there is no better time than now to begin building your credit history. But then I must warn you to be extremely careful not to abuse your credit card; if you know you can't discipline yourself, then I think you shouldn't get a credit card.

Before obtaining a credit card, do some research, and be sure to go for a card that offers: low-interest rate, no annual fees and reasonable grace period (i.e. the duration before which you should pay off the balance you owe without any charge). Once you have got your credit card, by the end of each month be sure to pay off the full balance you owe (not just the minimum payment), pay your bills on time to avoid charges, and review your credit account statement to detect any fraudulent transactions, if any exists. As much as you can, don't make the mistake of co-signing for somebody else's credit card to avoid any form of indebtedness. In addition to that, be careful about maxing out the limit on your credit card (for example, from $500 to $1500) just because you feel like spending more; let necessity be the only reason for pushing that limit.

Follow these words of caution, and you'll remain a happy owner of a credit card.

5. **Understand terms of service before entering any contract**:

This applies mostly to international students who are in a new country and are, therefore, oblivious to know how various systems in the country function. For such students, I advise that you always assume a difference in systems and culture until similarity is confirmed. One good example is in the area of purchasing a mobile phone plan. Telecommunication service varies across continents and even within countries in the same continent. Therefore, be sure to learn about any differences if at all any exist.

A friend of mine had told me a sad story of a mutual friend who had just migrated to a foreign country and was in her first year at university. Having little or no knowledge of the terms of service, this mutual friend had entered into a contract with a phone service provider and by the end of the first month, her bill, which was supposed to be less than $100, ended up becoming $2000. (Frightening? I know.) The reason for the astronomical bill figure was that this mutual friend had crossed the borderline of the coverage and agreement of her contract with the service provider; hence, she incurred additional charges for noncompliance.

In fact, I have heard similar first-hand stories of students who had fallen victims to the same trap. Hopefully, you are mindful to bypass that trap.

6. **Seek out money-making opportunities**:

As a student filled with energy and zeal, you can find employment opportunities starting from within campus to the outside world. Getting a part-time or co-op job are good prospects that you can explore as a student. With the extra money you get from a job, you can support yourself and not have to bother your parents all the time. But then try not to neglect your school work to focus more on a job, as this could have adverse consequences.

Eat healthily

Because of pressure for time and due to stress, the average student, who lives on campus or in a rented house, frequently eat at fast-food restaurants, preferring meals served there to meals prepared at home. But then, foodstuffs at most fast-food joints tend to be high in salt, white flour and sugar, all of which in his program "Thinking Big," Brian Tracy strongly advised should be fled from as much as possible; he tagged them – "the three white poisons." For one thing, taking those three substances in excess could lead to overweight and other health issues (especially if regular exercise is ignored as well). Eating healthy may be quite challenging but then cultivating the habit of eating unhealthy meals isn't preferable either, seeing that it could leave you unfit to go about your usual school business.

Even if you choose to desert the fast-food joints for expensive restaurants where healthier meals are served, you'll likely be spending a lot of money if you make this a habit.

Have problems with cooking?

It is very interesting how each time some students are asked why they indulge in eating junk foods, they respond with, "I am too lazy to cook" or "I don't feel like cooking" or "I can't cook." The truth of the matter is that if you consider eating healthy to be vital, then you'll find a way to stick to it. If you are unable to cook, you can always find out how to prepare your favourite meals by browsing Youtube.com or other websites from where you can learn. If you are still in high school, try to learn to cook some meals before leaving home for college or university; it will do you much good. I know of students who, as freshmen in university, knew only how to boil hot water for a cup of coffee, but after a couple semesters passed by, they became first-class cooks that their friends begged to live in the same house with them. Likewise, you can always learn to become a great cook.

Since weekdays usually are tight, cooking during the weekend is a good idea. You can prepare enough food (maybe 1-2 different meals, for example, fried rice then beans with plantain, etc.) and then refrigerate them to sustain you throughout the week; that is if you don't mind eating "unfresh" meals. For those who only eat right-off-the-pot, fresh meals, you'll have to plan more strategically.

As an undergrad, I observed that a couple of students were able to pull through with this strategy. You just can't afford to keep buying fast-food every single day of the week as this can negatively impact your pocket and possibly your health.

That being said, let's do a very quick exercise – shall we? Get a sheet of paper with a pen and write down the result to the following:

I.   How much does it cost to buy your favourite fast-food or meals at your favourite restaurant? (Maybe it is a plate of rice with chicken or sushi or noodles, whatever it is)

II. If you bought this food each day for an entire week, how much will that amount to?

III. Now suppose that you visited a local grocery store and purchased the recipe for preparing the same meals, the quantity that should last for one week or a couple of days. What will it amount to?

IV. Compare the result from II and III.

There is a very high chance that the amount obtained for II surpasses that of III (if you did the math correctly). This shows that you'll save money if you don't order fast food every day from restaurants and cook your meals instead. Of course, I am not in any way dissuading you from ordering delicious meals from restaurants; I only think that is it right that you be moderate about doing that and when you choose to do so, decide carefully.

Furthermore, by suggesting the above exercise, I am not implying that you feed on only one or two kinds of the meal for an entire week since that will be a sickly boring diet. The main purpose of the exercise is to show that you'll spend more money if you were to order meals each day versus if you were to prepare them yourself.

Nuggets on eating healthy

1. Adopt the Olympic diet:

Even if you don't plan on becoming an athlete, it is still worth eating like an athlete for the sake of staying in good shape. The Olympic diet comprises the following:

    a.   lean-source protein including meat, fish, chicken, eggs, dairy, beans, soy foods, nuts and many others

    b.   fruits & vegetables such as apples, bananas, grapes, tomatoes , broccoli, salads, and so forth

    c.   8 glasses of water per day

You can add to the list other foodstuffs that are rich in carbohydrate. The Olympic diet, being a balanced diet, will provide the vitality required by your body to function properly.

2. Don't skip breakfast:

Research shows that those who skip breakfast are more unmotivated, uninterested and irritable than those who don't. Besides that, there is evidence that individuals who miss breakfast are more apt to pack on weight compared to those who take breakfast quickly. The reason for this is that someone who doesn't eat in the morning will most likely binge in the afternoon; if this becomes a habit, the effect, in the long run, may not be admirable. Also, if you have been feeling drowsy at your morning lectures, then consider taking breakfast that's rich in fibre and carbohydrate as they'll help keep you more alert.[3]

3. Eat lightly:

Thomas Jefferson once wrote, "No one ever regretted eating too little after a meal." As much as possible, try not to overeat especially in the morning or late in the evening, so you don't get too sluggish that you snore in the middle of a lecture or fall asleep before completing your tasks for the day. Overeating leads to fatigue, but eating light keeps you agile and alert throughout the day.

Stay fit

Eating healthy is just as important as exercising regularly since both, to a high degree, determine your health and physical fitness. To maintain proper well-being, physical fitness experts recommend exercising for about 200-300 minutes per week which is about 30 - 60 minutes 3-4 times per week. Furthermore, studies have proven that the best time of the day to exercise is in the morning. One of the reasons for the claim is that there is evidence that those who carry out aerobic exercise early in the morning appear to be brighter, more creative, more alert and awake all through the day.[4] The simple explanation for this occurrence is that the cerebral cortex, the part of the brain that plays a key role in thinking, memory and decision making, gets stimulated by the influx of hyper-oxygenated blood during aerobic exercises.

Going to the campus gym in the morning may be quite a challenge especially if you have to do it alone. The good thing is that you can always get a workout even without working out at the gym. You can take a walk or jog around your neighbourhood, or do some weightless body exercises such as push-ups, sit-ups, mountain climbers, plank, amongst others exercises that will boost your pulse rate (consult google.com to learn more of the aerobic exercises, and how to perform them).

The weightless body exercises can be done right in your home, and they are right activities you can get started with. By the time you are about 20-30 minutes into your vigorous exercise, you'll notice a feeling of euphoria due to the release of endorphins by your brain; this is apparently the best feeling to begin the day with. In fact, back in my undergrad days, I always looked forward to my early morning workout sessions because, by the time I was done, I was set to dash out for lectures with lightning speed just like Usain Bolt.

Tips for staying fit

1. Get a workout buddy or join a group/team:

It can be difficult to remain consistent with your workout routine if you are in it alone. That is why it is suggested that you find someone to exercise with, if you can, especially when you are just getting started. You'll less likely give excuses not to work out and skip fewer exercise sessions if you have a buddy to accompany you, someone you are accountable to. The fact that you are accountable to your workout buddy will help you remain committed to your fitness; that is if you are really serious about staying fit. In short, the more workout buddies you have, the better (the more, the merrier).

During my undergrad days, a friend of mine who had lost a significant amount of weight began organizing workout sessions around campus. I was amazed by the commitment of the participants at those sessions as, mostly in the summer, they would meet up as early as 6 a.m., and sometimes in the evening to exercise for about an hour or two; this would continue all through an entire semester. At one time, I soon realized that not only did the participants meet up to exercise, but they also encouraged one another and did groceries together so they could monitor one another's food intake. That explained why each person looked forward to the next workout sessions. As you would expect, a good number of the participants reach their fitness goals as they remained consistent.

2. Make it a habit:

It takes motivation to begin a routine, but it takes discipline to remain consistent with it; discipline in itself reinforces habit formation, and it will be very useful in this area. The more you skip your workout routine, the higher your chances of never getting back to it. You can initiate some cues that will prompt your body to get set for the workout routine. For example, most people place their workout clothes on their bed right beside them so that it greets them when they wake up. In addition to that, some others also leave their workout shoes on the floor right by their bedside that they trip over their shoes when they jump out of bed (if you choose any of these, try not to skip your morning meditation time though). With these tactics, most people have been able to remain consistent with their morning exercise especially when they anticipate the end reward – the feeling of elation from the endorphins rush. Give it a shot!

Maintain a positive mental attitude

The saying that your attitude determines your altitude is a great truth that applies even to your school life. You are what you are and where you are because of the thoughts that you allow to creep into your mind. The wisest man who ever lived, King Solomon, put it this way, "... as he [man] thinks in his heart, so is he."[5] In short, we are a product of our thoughts.

Students, who think they can never ace a course, graduate on time or excel after graduation, will most likely not get disappointed except by some twist of faith. Always remember that the fact that you've failed a couple of times to achieve a goal doesn't mean that you are a failure; it only means that your plan or approach wasn't sound enough, and if you persist while maintaining a positive mental attitude, soon you'll be embracing your desired goal.

Whenever you commit to achieving worthy success - be it to complete a course with an A+, give a compelling presentation, win a tournament or competition, or graduate with a first-class (i.e. great distinction) – stay positive. Resolve not to quit because winners never quit and quitters never win. Also, have faith that you can do it, and apply yourself to work through challenges.

How to maintain a positive mental attitude

1. Make use of positive affirmations and autosuggestion:
Affirmations and autosuggestion are both age-old techniques that have been used to trick the subconscious mind, the mental driver, to action. The techniques entail writing down your desires and goals then repeatedly declaring them often enough till they get deeply ingrained into your subconscious mind. The subconscious mind, which comprises a huge portion of the mind, then works tirelessly to unite your behaviours with your emotionalized thoughts and desires. For example, suppose you are preparing for a big exam, a presentation or a competition, you can practice positive affirmation and autosuggestion by repeatedly declaring aloud the written statement of your goals; it can be - "I will ace my upcoming exam.", or "I will deliver an excellent presentation.", or "I will win that competition." If you want to keep it simple, you can use, "I can do this." Repeat the affirmations until they become a reality, and I am sure they will.

Keep your affirmations positive, personal and precise. Adding emotions to your affirmations will hype your self-confidence and more strongly influence your subconscious mind. In their book, "Success through a Positive Mental Attitude," Napoleon Hill and W.

Clement Stone recommend a daily dose of affirmation for positive self-suggestion; it should be declared whenever you feel sad, sick or down, and it is - "I feel healthy! I feel happy! I feel terrific!"

2. Apply positive, creative visualization:

Come to think about it, virtually everything that you've ever done in the physical world first took place in the mental world, your mind. Take, for example, the event of ordering a meal at a restaurant. Before starting out to the restaurant, you had already played the scene in your mind and had observed what you'd order, what the meal will look like and possibly smell like, how much you'll pay, and how you'll position yourself to enjoy the meal. Likewise, when working toward attaining success in any area, visualize yourself achieving that goal. This way you'll be blocking negative thoughts from entering your mind to discourage you.

As an undergrad student, one major area I worked to improve on was delivering presentations; I had enrolled in a course for that and sought opportunities to speak before groups. Whenever I prepared to give a presentation, I always visualized myself standing confidently before my audience, speaking with audacity as Martin Luther King Jr. did when he delivered his *"I have a dream"* speech. By the end of the actual presentation, I am usually not disappointed with the visualization technique; in fact, I still practice it till this day. (My presentation skill isn't 100% perfect though; I am constantly honing it.)

Whether you aspire to become the next Bill Gates, Oprah Winfrey or Albert Einstein, positive and creative visualization will be a great ally. Never forget – if you can think it, you can do it.

3. Run away from people with a negative attitude:

It is clear that the positive pole of a magnet gravitates toward the negative pole of a magnet, but two positives repel each other, and same is true for two negatives. In short, like poles repel while unlike poles attract. However, when it comes to maintaining a positive attitude, this law doesn't hold. Flee from students who possess a negative mental attitude; they are the same folks who speak or think negatively about themselves and are always pessimistic. Hang out with them too long and their negative attitude will, unfortunately, rub off on you.

The people you mostly hang around have a significant influence on your life that soon enough if care isn't taken, you begin to utter the same language they use as well as think and act the same way they do. Therefore, to maintain a positive attitude, remain in the gathering of positive-minded students.

4. Read and listen to inspirational materials:

You need a regular dose of inspiration to keep you mentally pumped up throughout each day. Listening to inspirational messages and reading inspirational books are great ways to stay motivated. I understand that you may already have a lot of textbooks to read that you can barely open up other books. You can invest in reading inspirational books especially during the holidays, or download audio books on your mobile device to listen to them, for example, while you commute. You can find a lot of inspirational and motivational media on Youtube. Remember that readers are leaders. The more you know, the better the decisions you make and, hence, the more desirable will be the quality of your life.

5. Change your attitude toward failure:

This is quite a tough one, yet it is very critical. Many times we see failure as a reason to quit and give up on a pursuit, but it ought not to be so. Failure is neither fatal nor final. It is, as Truman Capote put it, "… the condiment that gives success its flavour." On the road to success, you are apt to meet a couple of failures (I mean this in a positive way), but if you don't give up, you'll eventually achieve your desired success. The failures you encounter will only spur you to achieve outstanding feats if you learn from your mistakes and decide not to quit. Remember that

quitters never win and winners never quit even in the face
of defeat and failure.

Bombing the first midterm isn't the end.

Sometime in my second year of undergrad, I had enrolled in a
mandatory, core, theoretical and foundational math course which
was a nightmare for folks in my program. I admit that it started off
being a horror to me as well. I bombed the first midterm so badly
that I felt out of touch with, and almost beside, myself. I had the
option to drop the course like most of my study buddies, and close
friends did, but then I chose to hang on tight till the end. Even with
that failure and bombshell haunting my mind, I didn't lose grip on
a positive mental attitude; I still had my gaze fixed on my end goal
for that course.

For the remaining part of that semester after that bombshell, I
found myself putting in extra effort toward that course, solving
more problems, getting all the help I required by making my home
in the math centre and "lodging" in the prof's office; as a result the
prof and I became good buddies as housemates are. By the end of
that semester, I was thrilled I hit my target for that course.

Looking back at that experience, I am amazed by how I managed to
have pulled through that event. One thing I know for sure is that the
initial failure and setback I had encountered actually set me up for a
superb comeback and materialization of my end goal for that course.
But then the story would have sounded entirely different had I
dropped the course upon the initial failure.

From that experience, I learnt that every failure brings with it a
seed of equivalent success and that our failures have the potential
to propel us to achieve significant height. However, this can only
happen with a positive mental attitude.

Put them all together
The best time to begin cultivating these habits – getting involved

outside the classroom, managing your funds, eating healthy, staying fit, and maintaining a positive mental attitude – is now. Good habits, though, are hard to form but produce admirable results when mastered. On the other hand, bad habits are easy to form, challenging to get rid of when created, and their outcomes are usually not desirable. As mentioned earlier in this chapter, success and failure in these areas can trickle into your academic work. The great news is that these habits will prove useful to you even past the walls of the school, so you won't be wasting your time developing them.

In the next chapter, I'll discuss how you can prepare for the after-graduation phase as you approach the finish line of your school journey. You'll also learn how you can ensure to complete your school journey just as well as and, possibly, better than you began it.

Roll up your sleeves

1. Have you been eating unhealthy meals lately? Do you always buy food from restaurants? If so, how can you change that using the suggestions given in this chapter? (Remember that changing this will save you money and help keep you healthy)
2. Have you been eating a lot and doing little or no exercise? Do you exercise at all? How can you incorporate workout sessions into your weekly schedule so you can stay fit? (Morning is a good time.)
3. Do you have a monthly budget? Do you keep track of your expenses? Have you been spending more than you earn? Do you have a saving account at your bank? If you answered no to any of these questions, take some time to attend to what is required so you can answer in the positive.
4. Having identified the goals, you hope to accomplish, practice positive affirmation and visualization to keep your self-confidence and self-esteem high.
5. Resolve to cultivate good habits that will help you eat healthily, exercise regularly, spend your money wisely, save more money, and keep a positive mental attitude.

Part 3
Approaching the finish line

CHAPTER SEVEN

End strong, end well

*"If the beginning is well, you must
struggle not to fail for the beginning
and end must leave nothing pending."*
~~ Anonymous

f you have watched athletes sprint during the Olympics games, you'll observe that, to them, starting the race well is just as important as ending it well. Apart from that, taking a break or slowing down halfway on the tracks is not an option for an athlete who plans to end triumphantly. In fact, as the athletes draw near to the finish line, the race heats up the more as each person almost expends all his/her might to ensure a victorious ending. The same is true for your school journey. The level of effort with which you started the journey will seldom be sufficient to sustain you till the end; you'll have to boost it up because the challenges usually get tougher as you approach the finish line. However, the good news is that as the going gets tough, the tough get going. But this doesn't happen automatically and will require some conscious actions on your path to keep you on course till the triumphant end.

In this chapter, you'll discover useful tips on securing a dream job, writing a "killer résumé" and a captivating cover letter, getting prepared for a job interview, and pursuing graduate studies. But before proceeding with those, let's quickly look at how you may revitalize your focus along the school journey.

Pause to renew your focus and priorities

About midway on your school journey, you may have gotten involved in a couple of activities outside your academic work in an attempt to balance school life, which is fine. But then as you get near the finish line, say by your 3rd year, it helps for you to reassess your commitments to ensure that you aren't taking on more than you can handle while still pursuing your major academic end goals.

Let's say you had set a goal to graduate with distinction (or first-class as it is also called) by the end of your academic program; but then you are still an executive of the student union on campus, a president of a student club, a member of two departments at a charity organization, and probably holding two other roles elsewhere; that could be quite a lot of hats for your head.

As you draw closer to the end of your academic program, you want to disengage from activities that won't push you toward reaching your major final goals so you can summon more resources toward fulfilling your desired end. Look at it this way: suppose that you desire to graduate with a GPA of 3.0 (out of 4), for instance, but then you are still overweighed with other commitments that are unrelated to your overall goals, and as a result, you didn't hit your target. On the day of your graduation, you won't be excused for not obtaining 4.0 because of your involvement in many extracurricular activities.

The bottom line here is this: by about a year or two away from the completion of your program, try to cut down on your activities so you can concentrate more of your effort toward the achievement of your desired end goals.

Pause to smell your roses

Since the journey gets typically more challenging the farther you travel, there is a tendency to want to throw in the towel in the face of discouragement and disappointment. In times like that, it helps to revisit and recall your achievements and memories of good times from the earlier parts of the journey (think deeply – you have several of those). Refer back to those joyous experiences to remind yourself of the great milestones you've covered and of the great possibilities that lie ahead. The fact that you've gotten far is an indication that you are smart enough and are able to surmount the mountains in front of you. Remind yourself of these facts and move on – you were born to make it.

A strategic approach to winding up the school journey

Talking about winding up your school journey, you already know for sure that starting off well is just as important as ending well. A friend of mine, Ibukun Akinpelu, has some sage insights to share on how you can arrive at the end of your school journey with your end goals fulfilled. (At the time of writing, Ibukun is currently enrolled in MSc in Biochemistry at Western University in London, Ontario Canada, having graduated with a distinction in his undergraduate program). Here is what he has to share:

> In the final year of my undergraduate program, I chose to push myself to the limits of what I could do. I took a language course and a research thesis course. To some, these combinations may have seemed crazy, but I did it anyway. However, even as I pushed myself to the limit, I applied wisdom. I cut down on some of the extracurricular activities of which I partook and gave my best to the rest that remained. I also started looking into what I needed to do after my undergraduate the degree was fulfilled. I understood that undertaking a research thesis course

would be very demanding as would the Spanish language course also. I needed to ace both courses to better my chances of getting into medical school. Consequently, I made a list of all the clubs/groups I was a part of and used some criteria to cutdown those that I could do away with. For the criteria, I considered if I had been a part of that group for a while, if I was a leader in that group, and if it was important to my end goal. Towards the second semester of my research thesiscourse, I realized that I would have to put in a lot of time in the lab. And I was happy that I had made the decision to cut down my involvement in some of those extracurricular activities.

My advice to you is to "start well and finish better." In my first year of university, I did not partake in any extracurricular activities as I was trying to see what pace and study environment worked for me. In my fourth year, I chose to reduce the amount of extracurricular activities because I realized that even though they were important, they were not as important as my grades in the pursuit of my end goal (getting into med school). Every activity, in my opinion, should be accessed in the light of the end goal(s).

Applying this approach can help you focus all your attention on a few activities so you can excel at them instead of partaking in multiple activities and excelling at none.

Where do you go from here?

Reverend Edward A. Malloy once remarked, "A college degree is not a sign that one is a finished product but an indication that a person is prepared for life." In other words, neither college nor university is an end in itself; both are only a means to an end.

Your time in school is only a preparation for the next phase of your life. The earlier you begin thinking about the question - "Where do I go after I graduate?" - the higher will be your chances of making the right decisions when the time comes.

As you approach the finish line of your school journey, it helps to have a glimpse of what that next phase of life is as it will help you take the right steps that will eventually get you there. For example, if you plan to get a lucrative job after you graduate, it is necessary that you begin acquiring relevant skills that will prepare and distinguish you in the fiercely competitive job market.

Three main possibilities of what that next phase will include: securing a job, pursuing an advanced program, or starting up a business. Honestly speaking, saying that one option is better than the other is difficult since it all depends on individuals, their current conditions and life's goals. So then, what does that mean for you? I suppose it means that you shouldn't decide, for example, to pursue a Master's program simply because your best friend plans to do the same. Neither should you choose to enter the job market just because one of your study buddies chose to do the same. Given conditions such as availability of funds, family responsibilities, amongst others, you want to decide for yourself what option is best for you. It is ok to discuss with family members, friends, professors, or career advisers to get their opinions, but then at the end of it all, you have to take responsibility for the decision you make.

To help you decide on which one of those three options will suit you best, answering the following questions will be useful:

1. What interests me the most – engaging in advanced academic work, working in a company or being my own boss?

2. Am I financially buoyant enough to fund a graduate program or launch a business? Or, would I rather work to save up some money?

3. Do I have the qualifications and qualities required to excel? (For graduate school, the qualification will likely be a stipulated cut-off GPA from an undergrad study; while it can comprise technical and soft skills for the workplace and

entrepreneurial skills for starting up a business)

4. Which path will lead me toward achieving my long-term goals?

For the sake of simplicity, let's explore, in depth, the first two options.

Securing a dream job

If you are the kind of student who prefers practical, hands-on work over theoretical work, this option may be for you. Joining the job market offers you the opportunity to connect with professionals and to acquire relevant skills in the selected field. If you have co-op or internship experience, you'd have had a glimpse of what working after graduation looks like. (However, it is not the end of the world if you haven't yet experienced it either.)

In order to increase your chances of landing your dream job, you want to pay attention to the following:

1. Have a strategic entry plan into the job market:

Your goal is to get the most lucrative job that you are best qualified for, a job that you love. If you don't love it, you'll less likely be motivated to do well at it. Since the job market is already intensely competitive, you want to have a good entry strategy into it. To this end, I have three action steps for you to consider: One, discover about 3-5 organizations whose workforce you aspire to be a part of, then begin researching them. Two, find out what positions in those organizations you'd enjoy doing the most and determine what skills are required to excel at the positions. Three, begin acquiring those skills if you don't already have them.

Take note that the first two steps above don't have to follow that sequence; you can discover what positions interest you before beginning to explore what organizations you plan to work at. What is extremely important is that you know the exact positions you want and where you plan to find them.

As mentioned earlier, the job market is competitive, and for you to get what you want, you have to concentrate your effort. Businessman and motivational speaker, Nido Qubein once said, "Nothing can add more power to your life than concentrating all your energies on a limited set of targets." I am usually a bit concerned when I hear students say something like, "I just want any job" or "any job will do," especially when they are referring to a permanent job which they plan to remain at for a long time.

When one goes on job hunts with the mindset of getting "any job," finding the most lucrative job will likely be more challenging than if one has a definite target of the kind of jobs one wants. It may be understandable to make such statement about a temporary job, but not about a permanent job. Remember that for a permanent job, you may be sticking to it for quite a while, so you have to love it else you'd experience the feeling endured by an individual wearing an overly tight pair of shoes – that's right - it is the feeling of pain and discomfort.

Let's recap those three action steps: discover the top 3-5 organizations you aspire to work at, find out the positions that interest you and acquire the skills required to excel at those positions.

2. Present an attention-grabbing application:

On average, about 250 applications (i.e. 1 résumé and 1 cover letter per application) are submitted for each job opening in the corporate world. [1] As you know, only 1 application gets selected at the end of the hiring process for a particular position. Your goal is to make your application be the last one standing, and the good news is that it is always possible.

In your résumé, you give a history of your education, work experiences (both paid and volunteer positions), and accomplishments; whereas in your cover letter, you tell the hiring manager who you are, what you bring to the table, and why you are a good fit for the position and the company.

When writing a résumé and a cover letter, it is extremely crucial that you tailor them to match the job description (or job posting, as it is also called) for the position you are applying to. Nowadays, many companies employ the use of screening systems to filter job applications based on how well the résumé submitted match the given job description. This is especially true for positions that attract a huge number of applications that it becomes painful for the hiring team to handle. Basically, here is how it works: there usually are several buzzwords in each job description. And as many of these buzzwords are found on a candidate's application, the higher the candidate's chance of getting selected for the next stage of the hiring process.

3. Prepare well for job interviews:

Reaching the job interview stage in a hiring process usually means that your résumé and cover letter captivated the mind of the hiring manager (kudos!). Now, it is time for you to convince the hiring manager that you are the best fit for the position. As much as possible, don't wait until you get called up for a job interview before you begin thinking of or preparing for one. Ideally, you should begin preparing once you've declared yourself a job hunter. Be proactive about your job interview preparation just so you are not always under pressure as you hastily get ready for future interviews.

Writing an eye-catching résumé

Ideally, your résumé should be between 1-2 pages long, and the content should be as succinct as possible. A typical résumé contains the following sections: header, objective or profile summary (not mandatory), education, work experiences, volunteer experiences, skills, achievements, and interests (not mandatory).

Let's take a closer look at each section:

1. Provide an effective header:

The first couple of lines of your résumé contain your personal information. This should include your names, professional email address, and phone number. You want your names to stand out from the other text at least to give a good impression to your reader. Notice the way I had added "professional email address." As much as possible, avoid using email addresses such as drunkjones@hotmail.com, partyingkerry@aol.com, or you see anything weird with those email addresses? Create a new email address if you have to – it is worth the effort.

Whether or not one should include a home address on a résumé is a controversial topic. Some people believe that if you don't live locally, then you shouldn't include your home address as this could evict you from the hiring process. On the other hand, leaving off your home address on your résumé may give the recruiter the impression that you live in a different city. Personally, I don't think it's a bad idea to have a home address on your résumé. Furthermore, ensure that the information provided in the header is up-to-date.

Here is a sample header:

Chris T. White
1550 Yogi Drive Pittsburgh, Z0G 3M6 US
Phone: +1819-490-0990 Email: chriswhite@gmail.com

2. Highlight your educational qualifications:

Starting with the most recent till around Grade 10 or Year 4 of High School or Secondary School, present your educational qualifications which should include: name of school, the associated degree(s) or certificate, major (i.e. program of study), period of study (or expected year of completion if not completed yet), and Cumulative Grade Point Average (CGPA) if it is at least 3.0 out of 4 or its equivalent.

A sample should make this clear:

EDUCATION

Bsc Physics, Honors

Cambridge University, UK England– Degree expected, June 2020 **Cumulative Average**: 3.5 / 4

3. Outline your past experiences:

Write down any experiences you feel are relevant to the job you are applying for; these experiences can range from volunteer experiences, internship or co-op placements, part-time or full-time jobs, and projects or initiatives either within or outside your coursework. For each entry, include the title of the project or job role, the organization, time period and a short, 1-2 sentence-long description. Your description should begin with action verbs such as assisted, directed, managed, developed, maintained, led, and so forth. It is also a good idea to share a link to a website where you demonstrated the actual projects you have worked on if you have one.

Here is an entry for this section:

WORK EXPERIENCE

Graphic Designer (Co-op)

Sick Kids Toronto, ON, Canada   Summer 2013
* Designed the layout of a new Web portal
* Leveraged the power of Adobe Photoshop to create customized images for the portal
* Collaborated with healthcare specialists to come up with requirements for building clients' applications

4. Skills:

State the skills you possess that are related to the job you are applying to. These can include programming languages, applications, software or operating systems you are familiar with. Add a taste of creativity in presenting this section; you should consider classifying the skills so that the section looks organized and catchy.

Here is a sample:

TECHNICAL SKILLS

* **Programming/ scripting language:** SS TML, Java, JavaScript, PHP, hell.
* **Operating system:** ndroid, Ubuntu, Windows,
* **Software/ Application:** dobe Photoshop, Adobe Flash, Dreamweaver, Joomla, WordPress, MySQL, JQuery, Microsoft office (MS Word, Excel, PowerPoint)

5. Showcase your achievements:

List any academic or workplace awards, recognition or certifications you have earned to impress your reader. Mind you, you are not cocky by doing this. You are imply advertising yourself. After all, if you don' inform the reader about your accomplishments, he or she will never know.

HONOURS/AWARDS

* Outstanding Scholars Awards in Graphic Design
  Fall 2017   - Present
* Renewable Entrance Awards   Fall 2017 -Present
* School of Graphic Design Director Honour Roll (Dean's list)
  Fall 2017 -present
* Golden Key International Honor Society member
  Winter 2017
* Entrance Scholarship   Fall 2017 -Fall 2018

Optionally, you can have a section to mention your interests if you deem them relevant to the job you are applying to.

Composing the winning cover letter

The main aim of a cover letter is to convince the hiring manager to call you in for an interview so you can prove to him or her that you are the perfect match for the position you've applied for. Typically, your cover letter should be contained on one page and should be your best piece because you have only a few minutes to persuade your reader to call you in for an interview.

Here are some points to help you make that happen:

1. Address the reader appropriately:

In some cases, the job postings will specify the name of the person to whom the cover letter is to be addressed. In the case where no name is provided, refrain from referring to your reader as, 'To Whom It May Concern' since it is indirect and somewhat impersonal. Instead, you can use, 'Dear Hiring Manager' or 'Dear HR Manager.'

2. Have a powerful introduction:

Always bear in mind that the hiring manager may have quite a few cover letters to read. Therefore, your plan is to capture his or her attention right in your introductory paragraph. Don't bore them with the traditional paragraph that reads something like:

Dear HR Manager:

I am writing to inform you of my interest in the position of a Mechanical Engineer in your company.

I bet the HR Manager is tired of seeing that empty and cliché introduction. You want an introductory statement that will make your reader blurt out, "Now this is the kind of person I am looking for!" or "Wow! That is impressive!"

To achieve this effect, consider starting your cover letter with an expression of your passion or excitement for the position or the company. You can also start by highlighting some of your achievements. Here is an example:

Dear HR Manager:

It has always been my desire to revolutionize the world and to develop new technologies; this was one of my reasons for studying Computer Science with specialization in Software Engineering. I will be completing my degree this summer, and I believe that my strong academic knowledge, together with my co-op and volunteer experiences, make me a good candidate for this position.

3. **Demonstrate that you have the skills, don't just outline them:** Try not to repeat an outline of your skills since you already have that on your résumé. You want to select only those skills that are relevant to the position you are applying for and then, using examples, convince your reader that you genuinely possess those skills. For example, if a job posting requires good verbal and written communication skills, it is not enough to merely say,

"I have very good communication skills." You want to justify that statement by including where you had exhibited that skill as well as what you had accomplished with it. Here is an example:

> Furthermore, my strong verbal and written communication skills have been demonstrated in my everyday conversations with my co-workers, and in the presentation of my projects to our clients.

The skill doesn't have to be one that you had acquired while working at a company. It can also be one that you learnt on your own. In fact, mentioning that you acquired a skill independently outside school work tells your reader that you are proactive and take the initiative to advance yourself.

The bottom line here is this: looking at the job posting, for each skill asked for (of course, those that you possess), you want to prove to the reader that you've got it. By mirroring the keywords used in the job posting, not only are you demonstrating that you thoroughly reviewed it, but you are also increasing your chances of getting the interview.

4. Express willingness to learn:

No one knows it all, and your reader is aware of this truth. Hence, you always want to communicate your intention and willingness to learn even about skills you don't possess but were mentioned in the job posting.

Top tips for the job interview

Preparing for a job interview can be quite a hassle but with the before, during, and after-interview tips provided here, you should be fine.

Before the interview

1. Research the company and the job posting:

Once you know the company you'll be interviewing with, browse the company's website to learn more about it and the position you've applied for. Concerning the company, you want to find out what it deals in, who its competitors are, who its CEO is (trust me; some interviewers ask this question), and possibly what excites you about it (for example, maybe it is one of the big players in the industry). Besides that, since you applied for the job, you should be able to demonstrate how your skills and values fit well with the job requirements and company's vision.

2. Lookup sample interview questions:

Find out what kind of interview you'd be involved in – behavioural or technical interview – so you know how best to prepare. Some companies may organize two interview sessions, one solely behavioural-based and the other solely technical-based; other companies may have one interview session to cover both the technical and behavioural aspects. The best way to learn about what kind of questions to expect at a job interview is to discover what questions have been asked in the past. By visiting websites such as Quora.com, Glassdoor.com, and other career-based sites (google.com can direct you to the rest), you can get actual questions asked of job candidates who were interviewed for specific positions at various companies.

3. Rehearse your responses to the interview questions:

Once you have garnered enough interview questions, provide your own responses to them. Afterwards, rehearse how you would respond to the questions if an interviewer were to pose them to you. If possible, carry out mock interviews with a friend, family member or career adviser, where the other person plays the interviewer and you the interviewee; that will be an excellent way for you to get instant feedback on what to improve on; it could be your delivery method, eye contact or handshake. Nothing beats practice.

4. Apply the STAR technique:

When practicing your responses to interview questions especially for the behavioural questions, consider applying the STAR (Situation Task Action Result) technique. In essence, if you're asked to describe a specific past experience - for example, how you handled a difficult team member in a project or how you managed to complete a complex project or assignment – the STAR technique entails that you: start off by stating the situation, define what the required task was, tell what actions you took, and conclude with the end result. Having your responses in that form helps keep your thoughts straight, so you don't ramble and babble.

The more questions you rehearse, the higher your confidence level. Finally, prepare a few questions to ask the interviewer (some sample questions are supplied in tip #8).

5. Dress for success, dress to impress:

In her book "*Mind what you wear: The Psychology of Fashion,*" Karen J. Pine, Professor of Developmental Psychology at the University of Hertfordshire, clearly reveals how individuals' self-esteem and confidence are impacted by their dressing. According to her, the way we think and feel are really affected by the clothes we wear. For this reason, it is highly recommended that when going for an interview, your appearance be professional; specifically, business attire as it will help boost your self-image.

Make sure your clothes are neat and wear moderate cologne. Also, ensure that your hair is properly kempt, your breath is fresh, and your shoes are clean. Take the time to look at yourself in the mirror before heading out for the interview.

In addition, keep in mind that you want to leave a strong first impression on your interviewer right from the moment both of you meet; dressing professionally contributes a lot to creating that effect even though it may not guarantee you the job.

6. Be punctual:

Show up at the venue for the interview at least 10-15 minutes before the allotted time. This way you can calm your nerves down and familiarize yourself with the workplace environment. You don't want to rush in late, breathing heavily into the interview. Also, have copies of your résumé, cover letter and reference list, just in case any of them gets asked for. Finally, switch off your phone. The last thing you want to happen during the interview is for your phone to ring during the interview – that alone can warrant a red flag and prevent you from being hired.

During the interview

7. Comport yourself well and stay calm:

It's the moment you've been waiting for, and hopefully, your nerves are calmed down reasonably well. After you must have greeted your interviewer with a smile and a firm handshake, focus your attention on the interviewer and listen carefully to the questions you are being asked. Don't be afraid to request that a question be repeated or elaborated on; just don't do this for every question as it may mean you aren't paying attention.

Your responses should be on point, concise, and authentic.

Remember to apply the STAR technique especially for behavioural questions. Furthermore, sell yourself well by stating not only how your skills and experiences match the requirements of the position, but also how they will benefit the company - make it your goal to do this.

One more thing, if you get asked a question you don't know, instead of just responding with "I don't know what that is.", continue by adding, "... but I will be glad to research that." This way you'll be turning what seems like a negative event to a favourable opportunity to learn something new.

8. Ask questions:

Interviewers gauge interviewees' interest in a job based on whether or not interviewees ask questions. Perhaps you weren't clear about something the interviewer said earlier, or you learnt some interesting facts about the company and needed some more information – don't hesitate to ask the interviewer. Also, be sure to prepare some questions before the interview.

Here are some questions you could ask:
a. "What will a typical work day be like at this position?"
b. "What are the most challenging aspects of this position?"
c. "How does the company reward excellence in the workplace?"
d. "Do you have any concerns about my eligibility for this position that you want me to address?"
e. "What is the next phase of the hiring process after the interview?"

Those are only a few questions you can ask; try not to leave the interview without asking your interviewer a non-trivial question. Before leaving the interview room, be sure to thank the interviewer warmly for his or her time.

After the interview

9. **Reflect on your performance**:

It is imperative that you spend some time to examine how well you did at the interview. Ponder on questions you answered remarkably well and those you didn't, behaviors you thought were awkward (maybe you were always gazing at a picture on the wall that you were inattentive to the interviewer) and those you believed you deserve some interview points for. Determine what you plan to do differently in your next interviews and what you plan to discard.

Also, take time to seek out answers or responses to questions you were unable to answer satisfactorily or questions you couldn't answer at all. You never know what questions you'll get asked in the next interview; perhaps the same or similar interview questions.

Moreover, if you really want to perform better at interviews, then you probably don't want to miss this action step. By evaluating your performance at the end of each interview, you'll be tracking the growth of your interviewing skills. Consequently, you'll only get better and better at interviews because whatever you track improves.

10. **Don't forget the "Thank you" email**:

It is a good idea to send your interviewer a "Thank you" email after the interview, appreciating the individual for his or her time. This single act can be a tie-breaker, I have heard, so don't think it is entirely worthless. However, it doesn't guarantee that you'll get the job, but it doesn't hurt to be nice either.

Pursuing advanced studies (Graduate Studies)

Taking this path means you've decided to commit about another 2 – 7 years toward a higher level of education characterized by writing and reading research papers, conducting research sessions and seminars, and possibly attending academic conferences. These may sound tedious to some, but to others, it is fun (this is one way to find out if this option is truly right for you or not). Just like securing a job, pursuing a graduate program requires a couple of procedures which you should be mindful of.

Finding the right major and school

In Chapter 2, I walked you through a list of factors to consider when choosing a major (or program) and a school for a college or undergraduate degree. Let's recap:

When choosing the right major:
1) Identify your strengths and passions
2) Recall your future ambition (or career) and dream
3) Consider the next phase
4) Seek counsel

Factors to consider when selecting the right school are:
1) Admission requirements
2) Program availability
3) Reputation and Cost
4) Location

Interestingly, these factors are also relevant when choosing a major and a school for graduate studies. You may want to revise that chapter if needed.

The program / major

When selecting a graduate program, you want to go for a major that interests you as well as one that is more specialized than broad. This is unlike an undergraduate program. For instance, suppose you are studying Psychology in your college or undergraduate program, then for your graduate program, you may have to narrow down to one of the branches of psychology such as biological, clinical, counselling, developmental, experimental, or social psychology; that is if you choose to stick to the field of psychology.

Besides that, have an idea of what the next stage is after you complete your graduate program - a Ph.D., a job or a business. Having knowledge of the next stage will help you focus on acquiring the skills and experiences that'll be required for moving forward. For example, if, after completing your graduate program, you plan on getting a job that is more inclined toward research and theory application, then you know to pay more attention to research and application of theory during your graduate program.

The school

When choosing the right school, be aware of the department's admission requirements, for example, prerequisite courses, cut off for grade point average, and so forth. No admission will be granted students who don't meet those requirements. If going to graduate school is your plan, then find out what these admission requirements are so you can work toward fulfilling them. In addition, take into account the location of the school. Some individuals prefer schools sited in quiet cities versus those in busy ones.

Furthermore, when researching graduate programs at different schools, remember that the end goal is to select a professor whose research work interests you. Note down relevant facts about your research as those will come in handy when writing your application.

Admissions experts recommend that you begin this process at

least 6 months before rolling out your application for grad school [3]; doing this will save you from rushing in the last minutes and making grave mistakes. Apart from doing your own research, seek advice from your undergraduate professors, academic counsellors, grad students in your school and experts in your field of interest. Don't try to work this out alone.

Applying for grad studies

Once you are sure you've got the right major and the right school, proceed immediately to apply while bearing in mind the application deadlines. As with the job market, entry into graduate school is competitive; hence, it behooves you to submit a strong and well-written application to increase your chance of getting admitted into the program of your choice.

The basic submission requirements for graduate school tend to be similar across schools; they include:

1. **Application form**:

    It is meant to provide basic personal information such as candidate's name, contact info, and education history.

2. **Personal statement**:

    This essay reveals the candidate's background, values, skills, personal challenges, goals, and motivation for applying to the graduate program. Here is where the candidate tries to convince the admission board that he or she is an excellent fit for the program based on his or her experiences and passion.

3. **Statement of purpose**:

    As the name implies, this essay spells out the candidate's purpose for applying to the graduate program; its primary focus is to emphasize why exactly the candidate chose the specific program. Here is where the candidate expresses his or her fascination for the work of the selected professor, and how the professor's work tallies with his or her research goals.

4. Transcripts:

The transcript will inform the admission committee of the kind and difficulty of the courses the candidate has taken with the corresponding grades, as well as the candidate's GPA at the undergraduate level.

5. Letter of recommendations:

These are reference letters written by faculty members with whom the candidate is well acquainted. The more recognized the writer of the letter is, and the more positive appraisals are written about the candidate, the higher the candidate's chances of getting accepted into the program. Here is why you should be nice to faculty members; you never know whom you'd need to write a recommendation letter for you.

6. Standardized tests scores:

These are standard tests meant to assess candidates' skills in areas including writing, reading, reasoning (quantitative and verbal), and sciences. The most common of such tests are General Management Admission Test (GMAT), Graduate Record Examination (GRE), Medical College Admission Test (MCAT), and Law School Admission Test (LSAT).

Again, it is highly suggested that students begin working on their application as early as about 6 months before the deadline.

The statement of purpose and personal statement should be revised at least by a faculty member before the application is submitted.

When it comes to financing the graduate studies, which can be expensive, look out for the availability of funding and financial aids at the school you plan to attend. This can be in the form of scholarship, bursaries, research assistantship and work-study program.

Top 10 skills/attributes to have as a fresh graduate

Based on research undertaken by notable career and professional development organizations such as National Association of Colleges and Employers (NACE) and PayScale[3], I have pulled together ten solid skills or attributes that fresh grads should have under their belts. These skills will prove very beneficial to you regardless of what path you choose to walk after you graduate.

1. **Time management and multitasking**:

    The ability to make the best use of your time, given a bunch of tasks is a very useful skill to have. You are probably used to working on about 3-4 different assignments or papers simultaneously and still getting all the work done on time and well, hopefully. Being able to do this is a good sign that you are getting yourself ready for the real world where you will have to juggle a couple of tasks and meet quite a number of deadlines.

2. **Interpersonal and teamwork**:

    It is almost impossible to complete a complex and worthy project without having to work with and get along well with others. Irrespective of where you end up as a new grad, you'll have to collaborate with other individuals, for example, manager, team member, business partner, or subordinate, depending on where you end up. If you are having a hard time working agreeably with a team member and will like to enhance your strength in this area, be sure to visit "Handling that big project" on Chapter 6 for more info.

3. **Communication**:

The world is always looking for individuals who are able to articulate their thoughts clearly both verbally and in writing. This skill has distinguished most of the leaders in the industry from their peers. Interestingly, a number of students shy away from this area, but I challenge you to develop and hone your writing and presentation skills, and I promise you'll be really glad you did. Taking courses in writing and speech communication will be a huge step in the right direction.

4. **Planning and prioritization**:

There will always be a thousand tasks you can complete in a single day and your ability to prioritize these tasks is critical. Apparently, that's because not all of those tasks have the same level of urgency and importance; so you'll need to determine the high-value tasks and then complete them before moving onto the next most important tasks. With planning and prioritization, you'll be sure to complete the most important tasks first and get the most returns for your efforts.

5. **Decision-making and problem-solving**:

These are valuable skills in any organization especially since problems abound just about everywhere. The best decisions are usually made based on facts and experiences and not based on guesswork. Besides that, setting yourself apart as a problem-solver will mark you as an invaluable asset wherever you go and will open doors of opportunities for you.

6. **Technical proficiency**:

This is basically the possession of specialized knowledge and skills which will eventually be required in related professional roles. For example, a computer science major who has good coding and problem-solving skills or a math major who is a whiz at calculations will be said to be technically proficient in their field. Try not to run away from core courses in your program as they will equip you with the foundational technical knowledge you require to excel in your field. Engaging in co-op and internship is a good way to toughen your muscles in this area.

7. Proficiency with computer programs:

This may seem surprising, but then come to think about it – in which one industry (as in healthcare, automobile, engineering, education, and so forth) isn't a computer in use? The answer is - virtually none. Therefore, apart from learning skills related to your field, it is a good idea to seek out computer skills that are relevant to your field. Doing this will give you an edge over your peers who stick strictly to learning only skills in their own field.

8. Leadership:

Leaders are known to possess admirable qualities such as responsibility, diligence, charisma, loyalty, amongst many others. These qualities are required to advance organizations; hence, the essence of this skill and that's why the demand for leaders is higher. Leadership is also a measure of the ability to lead and influence others. A good way to strengthen your muscle in this area, while in school, is to seek out leadership positions on campus or at the community you belong to, for example, a church, not-for-profit organization or another societal group.

9. Quantitative data analysis:

Simply put, this is the ability to describe an event or occurrence, having studied some numerical representation of such event or occurrence. It is a technique for making sense of data representations. This also entails possessing knowledge of data analysis software programs such Microsoft Excel, R, SPSS and/or other data analysis tools. Taking courses in Stats and Math can help you hone this skill too.

10. Strong work ethics:

With this attribute, you'll go places because it is very vital to the success of any organization. Possessing strong work ethics comprises the following [4]:

a. Professionalism in the areas of dressing and dealing with others.

b. Respectfulness to others especially in times of intense pressure.

c. Dependability in regards to keeping to one's word.

d. Dedication to excellence in the completion of assigned tasks.

e. Determination to breaking through hurdles of challenges at work.

f. Accountability for one's actions with the corresponding results, as well as for one's mistakes, i.e. no excuses or blame game.

g. Humility in being teachable while learning from others and leading by example.

Focus on building these skills/attributes, and you'll be boosting your chances of succeeding in the fiercely competitive world out there.

Wrap up

Obviously, securing a job and pursuing graduate studies are not the only options available to you after you graduate. You may have an entrepreneurship spirit and so desire to start up your own company or do freelancing; just follow your heart and be sure to get guidance on the path you choose. Do your best and don't settle for anything less.

Hopefully, after going through this chapter, you should now have a good idea of what you want to do after graduation. I wish you all the best with that.

It is painful sometimes to learn from our own experience, but then it is safer when we learn from the experiences and advice of others. The next chapter contains helpful advice from people who have traversed this school journey ahead of you.

Roll up your sleeves

1. Reassess your commitment to activities outside of your academic work. Are those activities eating much of your study time and effort? If so, take action to do something about that.

2. What do you plan to do after you graduate - work or pursue advanced studies or start your own company? Take some time to reflect especially when you are about one or two years away from completing your degree.

3. Getting set for a job interview? Remember to follow through with the "Top tips for the job interview" in this chapter.

4. Need an idea of what the requirements are for graduate studies? See "Applying for grad studies" in this chapter.

BONUS CHAPTER

61 wisdom nuggets for your school journey

"While it is wise to learn from your experience, it is wiser to learn from the experiences of others."
~~ Rick Warren

I really want you to get as much advice, perspectives, and tips around the theme of the book - all-round success; so I reached out to some academic advisers and high-achieving students from universities across the globe; most of the students are graduates now, by the way. They have given their best advice which they would typically reserve for close friends and families.

Before you begin the journey
1. Decide that failure or dropping out is not an option.
2. Commit your ways to God and do not forget who you are.
3. If you are thinking of a college or university to apply to, don't let your parents do all the work or take you to an agency to fill the same application you could have completed in a couple hours all by yourself. (This applies mostly to international students.)
4. Do your research and don't just pick any school or program of study because your friends chose the same.
5. The choice of courses and program of study must be determined

based on your personal interests, academic strengths and career goals.

6. Meet with an adviser to register for courses if registering seems difficult at first. But trust me, you'll get the hang of it soon enough.

7. You should prepare yourself physically, mentally and spiritually before starting out on this journey.

8. Before you begin, ask yourself this question, "What do I want to achieve by going to college or university?"

9. Design a plan revealing what you wish to achieve and how you desire to achieve them.

10. Knowing what you want to do from day 1 will help you choose the right courses and electives to take as you progress in your college or university career.

11. For 1st year students, it is a good idea to live on-campus at first, if you can afford it. This will really help you to meet new people, get connected to the campus and get involved in activities very quickly.

12. For international students especially, look out for: the availability of scholarships, how likely it is to get a permanent residency after you are done with schooling (if that's your plan), the job prospects for the degree you are applying for in that country, and many other factors that are worth considering when picking a country, school and program of study.

13. Do not hesitate to ask questions or seek counsel regarding your choice of program or school.

14. When you eventually find a school, while applying, don't be afraid to call the school's admissions office if you have any questions. They are very open to answering questions. Also, most schools have an International Student Office that caters to the needs and questions of international students. Call and ask

questions. (This applies to international students.)

While into the journey

1. Develop a discipline to adhere to a specific study schedule.
2. Apart from what happens in class, be sure to read up additional materials in the library or online.
3. Determine never to give up until you understand the content being taught at lectures.
4. Study hard and don't miss classes if you can help it.
5. Ask your professors what you could have done to earn better marks after your test papers are received.
6. Don't ever be afraid or anxious, especially when you have a test or exam. Learn to control your nerves.
7. Don't dwell on a test, especially if you cannot change the outcome.
8. Don't leave studying for tests till the night before. That's an excellent way to destroy your GPA.
9. Take at least 4 days to a week to prepare for a midterm or final exam.
10. Choose to study weeks beforehand so that while others are studying and cramming, you have the time to go over those little things that distinguish an A from an A+.
11. Complete every piece of homework given even if not graded.
12. Review your lecture notes weekly and make notes of any questions you have.
13. Make good use of office hours offered by professors and teaching assistants. Take advantage of those. They are great ways to get help in difficult courses and to get to know your prof better. (How do you think a lot of students get good reference letters for graduate school or jobs?)
14. Whenever there is anything interfering with your ability to

succeed, be sure to determine quickly what this is and seek out assistance, if necessary, to resolve the issue as soon as possible.

15. Look out for scholarships. You have a good chance if you have a good GPA. Demonstrate that you are a good student and write an appealing application.

16. Don't procrastinate or do things at the last minute.

17. Don't be a loner. Go out, meet people, and make new friends not just people from your own country or culture.

18. Get involved in events and happenings on campus; it is another great way to meet people and fill up the 'Volunteer' section of your résumé.

19. Tell me about your friends at college. Do they add value to you? Choose your friends wisely.

20. The projections you made prior to entering college or university do not necessarily translate into reality. Things may turn out differently so be adaptable.

21. Acquire leadership skills from stalwarts or mentors who are passionate about leadership.

22. Don't insist on only a single way of performing a task. Make sure you listen to and weigh the opinions of others.

23. Ask questions. For an international student, it is a new country, environment, and a new school, so it is impossible to know everything just all at once. Of course, Google is certainly your best friend, but there are some things that you just need to ask someone to know.

24. Besides academic pursuit, it is crucial to keep up the physical exercise on a regular basis. Your health always ranks one of the tops among all other goals you have throughout your life.

25. Keep in touch with your friends and expand your network of friends.

26. Join the co-operative education program (i.e. co-op). It is a great

way to acquire real-life experience while earning some cash even before you graduate.

27. Don't engage in activities that are against your belief or code of conduct.

28. Don't allow your decisions to be easily influenced by friends or colleagues.

29. Someone once told me that you only go to college once in your lifetime; so it's up to you to either make it fun and exciting or boring and lonely.

When wrapping up the journey

1. Keep track of how many courses you require to graduate, how many you have already taken and how many you have left. You don't want to be in school for an extra year or two, of course, unless you can afford it.

2. At around your second year or even first year, start thinking of what you want to do with your degree when you graduate and slowly work towards that.

3. If you want to go to a professional school such as Med school or Law school, start researching schools with their requirements. Figure out the following: are international students accepted into the program? What prerequisite courses are required? Do you need to write any exams to get into the program? It sounds like a lot, but it really helps if you start early and just have a list posted somewhere and slowly work through them. (Note: Talk to people who have gone through the process before you.)

4. If you want to apply to grad school, if research-based work is your thing, start working in research labs to help you hone the skills necessary for that program. Your supervisor is almost always a wonderful reference source as well.

5. Keep a good eye on your résumé, especially if you're applying for

jobs after you complete your degree. Start looking at the skill sets and experiences that companies are looking for regarding the position you want to apply for. Develop those skills, gain those experiences and make connections (mostly through summer internships and jobs).

6. Many universities offer career workshops, so look out for those as they are usually very informative (plus you get free food at some of them).

7. There are career advisers you can go to who'll guide you on the right path. Don't worry; you have lots of available help if you would only take advantage of them.

8. Having internship experience on your résumé would help a lot when you look for a full-time job after graduation.

9. Begin to distribute your résumé to prospective employers early enough if you plan to secure a job after graduation.

10. Spend some time improving your job search and interview techniques as well as your résumé and cover letter writing skills.

11. Approach your job search based on a strategy that meets your short-term and long-term goals.

12. Don't overly depend on the government or private companies for employment. You should adopt the mind of an entrepreneur.

13. While you should continuously seek out career advice during your program, an extra emphasis should be put on this aspect at least one year before you graduate. Also, it is essential to learn at this time what options are available to you to continue your education.

14. It helps to cut down on some extracurricular activities that you are involved in, so you can give your best shot to the rest that matter most.

15. The university experience is not all about academics; it is also about connecting with people and gaining the most experience

possible.
16. Encourage others who are yet to get to the level you are.
17. Stay away from people who try to belittle your potentials.
18. Be yourself, be confident, have fun and good luck!

Those are enough sage words to guide you through your school journey. You are in charge of your academic career; no one else is and should be. So, step up to the wheel of your school life and ride on till you arrive at your desired destination.

Conclusion

"The objective of education is to
prepare the young to educate themselves
throughout their lives."
~~ Robert Maynard Hutchins

I am glad you made it to the end; it is evident that you are a winner. (By the way, you didn't just skip all the way here – right?) I want you to remember this one thing: no one is smarter or better than you, per se. If a student performs better than you in an area, it is because that person knows and does something you don't know and don't do. Once you learn and apply what those "secrets" are, you'll be surprised by how much your performance will get boosted. Fortunately, many of those "secrets" have been revealed in this book, and I believe that by practicing them you'll not only achieve the all-round success you dream of but also you'll maximize your time spent in university or college.

At this point, you must have added new solid techniques to your arsenal of ideas, and you should be ready to apply them to respective areas of your school life. As a way of recapping and as promised in the introduction, you have gained tips and insights on how to:

- Choose the rigt major, school and courses
- Take the most of the available resources on campus
- Get SMART goals and map out strategies to achieve them
- Study like an 'A' student
- Write effective papers
- Ace your exams
- Deliver a powerful presentation
- Balance the academic and on-academic areas of your school life
- Secure your dream job
- Pursue a post-graduate degree

By implementing the myriad of concepts and ideas shared in the pages of this book, you'l put your academic career on the fast track For resources on cover letter and résumé and academic paper, visit https://www.allroundachievers.com under the "Resources" menu.

I believe that you possess the intelligence, abilities and talents required to achieve the ll-roundsccess that you desire. Take action right away!

I   wish you all the very best. Godspeed!

REFERENCES

Chapter 2

1. Nelson, L. (2013, June 20). The Bennett Hypothesis Returns. Retrieved 7 January 2017, from <https://www.insidehighered.com/news/2013/06/20/bill-bennett-writes-new-book-whether-college-worth-it>

Chapter 3

1. UK Council for International Student Affairs (2008).Planning and running orientation programs for international students, 13. Retrieved 17 October 2017, from <https://www.englishuk.com/uploads/assets/members/publications/orientation.pdf>
2. Owusu, T. et al (2014). Orientation impact on undergraduate students in University of Cape Coast (Ghana), 134. Retrieved 17 October 2017, from <http://www.academicjournals.org/journal/IJEAPS/article-full-text-pdf/A95911446966 >

Chapter 4

1. (2006, March 15). Harvard Business School Goal Story. Retrieved January 2, 2017, from http://www.lifemastering.com/en/harvard_school.html

Chapter 5

1. Klemm W. Ph.D. (2012, January 14). To Cram or Not to Cram? That Is The Question. Retrieved 2 January 2017, from <https://www.psychologytoday.com/blog/memory-medic/201201/cram-or-not-cram-is-the-question>
2. Patel N. (2014, December 11). When, How, and How Often to Take a Break. Retrieved 17 October 2017, from <https://www.inc.com/neil-patel/when-how-and-how-often-to-

take-a-break.html >

3. Gallo C. (2013, May 16). How Warren Buffett And Joel Osteen Conquered Their Terrifying Fear Of Public Speaking. Retrieved 9 January 2017, from <http://www.forbes.com/sites/carminegallo/2013/05/16/how-warren-buffett-and-joel-osteen-conquered-their-terrifying-fear-of-public-speaking/#43ecef39352a>

4. Brody M.(1999). Capture an Audience's Attention: Points on Posture, Eye, Contact and More. Retrieved 11 January 2017, from <http://www.presentation-pointers.com/showarticle/articleid/17/>

5. Successful Group Projects. Retrieved 12 January 2017, <http://www2.le.ac.uk/offices/ld/resources/study/group-projects>

Chapter 6

1. Tracy B. (2010). No excuse: The power of self-discipline, pp.191

2. Anne (2013, April 3). 10 reasons why you shouldn't skip breakfast. Retrieved 6September 2016, from <http://www.activebeat.com/diet-nutrition/10-reasons-why-you-shouldnt-skip-breakfast/>

3. Tracy B. (2010). No excuse: The power of self-discipline, pp.249

4. New King James Version Bible. Proverbs 23:7

Chapter 7

1. Economy P. (2015, May 5). 11 Interesting hiring statistics you should know. Retrieved 21 November 2016, from <http://www.inc.com/peter-economy/19-interesting-hiring-statistics-you-should-know.html>

2. The Daily Muse Editor. 31 Attention Grabbing Cover Letters Examples. Retrieved 22 November 2016, from

<https://www.themuse.com/advice/31-attentiongrabbing-cover-letter-examples>

3.   Klebnikov S. (2015, July 5). What Employers Are Looking For When Hiring Recent Grads. Retrieved 30 March 2017, from <https://www.forbes.com/sites/sergeiklebnikov/2015/07/06/what-employers-are-looking-for-when-hiring-recent-college-grads/2/#7e0aaf7d2f08>

4.   Whitmore J.(2015, September 1). 7 Elements of a Strong Work Ethics. Retrieved 30 March 2017, <https://www.entrepreneur.com/article/250114>

Thank you

Thank you for reading my book. If you found it helpful please take some time to leave a review online. I will really appreciate!

Made in the USA
Columbia, SC
14 February 2020